CORPORATE SOCIAL PERFORMENCE IN INDIA WITH SPECIAL REFERENCE TO COMPANIES ACT, 2013.

CORPORATE SOCIAL PERFORMENCE IN INDIA WITH SPECIAL REFERENCE TO COMPANIES ACT, 2013.

DR. PRATISHTHA YADAV

This book is dedicated to my Beloved Daughter **Runjhun (Ruchita Yadav)** & my nephwe **Dhruv (Dev Yadav)**. Thanks for making our family complete.

"No one will ever know the strength of my love for you.
After all, you're the only one who knows what my heart sounds like
from the inside."

Contents

Preface

Corporate social responsibility has several façades, and also known as *corporate responsibility, corporate citizenship, responsible business, sustainable responsible business (SRB), or corporate social performance,* is a system of corporate self - directive assimilated into a business model. Corporate Social Responsibility guidelines would act as a built-in, self-regulating tool whereby business would inspect and safeguard their consecration to law, ethical standards, and international models and consider being highly useful in the emerging business set-up. Business activities produce both positive and negative externalities for both society as well as environment also. Thus, the story of business and society rotates around how businesses would generate more positive externalities by abating negative externalities.

By the end of the 20th century, business grew to super size, accumulated wealth and had become centers of power. They influenced both the political system and governments in a great way. Their intrusive behavior in the political affair and undue influence on society lead to the great protest from several pressure groups for being too large, along with being anti-social. This brutal attack obligated business executives and owners to realize that they cannot remain indifferent, unsympathetic, and unresponsive to society. Thus, they owe some duty and accountability towards society and it was felt that apart from profit, enterprises should also incline towards social causes. Therefore, various initiatives has been adopted by many corporations in this line for instances, in Europe, steel giant Andrew Carnegie initiated the move by donating maximum of his wealth for education, charitable social causes. Another leading industrialist Henry Ford a well known auto giant, formulated health and recreation programs for his employees. This set the notion and business leaders started coming out of the shell of revenue to move closer to social causes and societal welfares.

On contrary, emphasis can also be made to Indian Companies who believe in corporate social responsibility. Most important names in Indian Corporate Social Responsibility are Birla Group, Bajaj Group, Tata Sons (who operates six trusts distributing approximately Rs.120 crores), etc. Lupin Human Welfare and Research Foundation (LHWRF), is an NGO run by Lupin Pharmaceuticals, which has put 120 schools, provided drinking water facilities in 80 villages and helped 25,000 people living below poverty line.

It is common accord that business must make such policies, include such technology and take such decision, which do not adversely affect society. Society expects enterprises to be more accountable and diligent. Corporate Social Responsibility is a global expectation that requires a comprehensive strategic response from business companies.

Our Constitution was also laid with an objective of one man equals one vote, equals one value. However the socio-economic realities of the country still have a long way to go to match this vision of independent India where today there are many first among equals. The country presently is under extreme discussion of developmental growth versus welfare based development. Thus, our political realities and our economic senses are at turning point.

Every single major policy initiative in this country has been driven with a standpoint that an overwhelming concern for the disadvantaged and marginalized, a multidimensional view of poverty and human deprivation, the focus on our fundamental rights and the need to expand opportunities while ensuring its equal distribution are fundamental for achieving strong human development. But disparity, inequality and the growing divide in our societies define our existence today. The inclusion of the Corporate Social Responsibility mandate under the Companies Act, 2013 is an attempt to supplement the government's efforts of equitably delivering the benefits of growth and to engage the Corporate World with the country's development agenda.

In nutshell, Corporate Social Responsibility (CSR) is the new buzzword in the modern age, and today, almost all big companies have specific guidelines on Corporate Social Responsibility. The business houses consciously engaged in efforts to give something back to society.

This dissertation aims to provide exploratory nature of research work on all aspect of Corporate Social Responsibility including its evolution in India, theoretical perspective, societal benefit, social reporting, and its changing dimension in light of New Companies Amendment Act, 2013. This dissertation is organized into six chapters, of which the 'Introduction' is the first chapter, which deal with the background and the growing concern of the Corporate Social Responsibility globally as well as in India with the windfall of globalization.

Further, Chapter 2 of the dissertation explores the evolutionary aspect of the term Corporate Social Responsibility in the world and in India. Third chapter identifies the concept of Corporate Social Responsibility along with its meaning, definitions, elements, importance and relevancy of it in today's world. Further, this chapter will also explore with the globally accepted guidelines relating to Corporate Social Responsibility. Thereafter, fourth chapter deals with the plan to integrate Corporate Social Responsibility in a legal framework in India by putting emphasis on a New Companies (Amendment) Act, 2013 which deals with the mandatory provisions of CSR in India. Similarly, fifth chapter explores the CSR practices in a Corporation in accordance with Companies Act, 2013, along with its implementations as required by them.

Lastly, Chapter sixth, of this dissertation deals with the conclusions reached along with the relevant suggestions.

Researcher hopes this dissertation will be helpful in understanding the policies relating to Corporate Social Responsibility with special emphasis on the New Companies Amendment Act of 2013.

Corporate social responsibility has several façades, and also known as *corporate responsibility, corporate citizenship, responsible business, sustainable responsible business (SRB), or corporate social performance,* is a system of corporate self - directive assimilated into a business model. Corporate Social Responsibility guidelines would act as a built-in, self-regulating tool whereby business would inspect and safeguard their consecration to law, ethical standards, and international models and consider being highly useful in the emerging business set-up. Business activities produce both positive and negative externalities for both society as well as environment also. Thus, the story of business and society rotates around how businesses would generate more positive externalities by abating negative externalities.

By the end of the 20th century, business grew to super size, accumulated wealth and had become centers of power. They influenced both the political system and governments in a great way. Their intrusive behavior in the political affair and undue influence on society lead to the great protest from several pressure groups for being too large, along with being anti-social. This brutal attack obligated business executives and owners to realize that they cannot remain indifferent, unsympathetic, and unresponsive to society. Thus, they owe some duty and accountability towards society and it was felt that apart from profit, enterprises should also incline towards social causes. Therefore, various initiatives has been adopted by many corporations in this line for instances, in Europe, steel giant Andrew Carnegie initiated the move by donating maximum of his wealth for education, charitable social causes. Another leading industrialist Henry Ford a well known auto giant, formulated health and recreation programs for his employees. This set the notion and business leaders started coming out of the shell of revenue to move closer to social causes and societal welfares.

On contrary, emphasis can also be made to Indian Companies who believe in corporate social responsibility. Most important names in Indian Corporate Social Responsibility are Birla Group, Bajaj Group, Tata Sons (who operates six trusts distributing approximately Rs.120 crores), etc. Lupin Human Welfare and Research Foundation (LHWRF), is an NGO run by Lupin Pharmaceuticals, which has put 120 schools, provided drinking water facilities in 80 villages and helped 25,000 people living below poverty line.

It is common accord that business must make such policies, include such technology and take such decision, which do not adversely affect society. Society expects enterprises to be more accountable and diligent. Corporate Social Responsibility is a global expectation that requires a comprehensive strategic response from business companies.

Our Constitution was also laid with an objective of one man equals one vote, equals one value. However the socio-economic realities of the country still have a long way to go to match this vision of independent India where today there are many first among equals. The country presently is under extreme discussion of developmental growth versus welfare based development. Thus, our political realities and our economic senses are at turning point.

Every single major policy initiative in this country has been driven with a standpoint that an overwhelming concern for the disadvantaged and marginalized, a multidimensional view of poverty and human deprivation, the focus on our fundamental rights and the need to expand opportunities while ensuring its equal distribution are fundamental for achieving strong human development. But disparity, inequality and the growing divide in our societies define our existence today. The inclusion of the Corporate Social Responsibility mandate under the Companies Act, 2013 is an attempt to supplement the government's efforts of equitably delivering the benefits of growth and to engage the Corporate World with the country's development agenda.

In nutshell, Corporate Social Responsibility (CSR) is the new buzzword in the modern age, and today, almost all big companies have specific guidelines on Corporate Social Responsibility. The business houses consciously engaged in efforts to give something back to society.

This dissertation aims to provide exploratory nature of research work on all aspect of Corporate Social Responsibility including its evolution in India, theoretical perspective, societal benefit, social reporting, and its changing dimension in light of New Companies Amendment Act, 2013. This dissertation is organized into six chapters, of which the 'Introduction' is the first chapter, which deal with the background and the growing concern of the Corporate Social Responsibility globally as well as in India with the windfall of globalization.

Further, Chapter 2 of the dissertation explores the evolutionary aspect of the term Corporate Social Responsibility in the world and in India. Third chapter identifies the concept of Corporate Social Responsibility along with its meaning, definitions, elements, importance and relevancy of it in today's world. Further, this chapter will also explore with the globally accepted guidelines relating to Corporate Social Responsibility. Thereafter, fourth chapter deals with the plan to integrate Corporate Social Responsibility in a legal framework in India by putting emphasis on a New Companies (Amendment) Act, 2013 which deals with the mandatory provisions of CSR in India. Similarly, fifth chapter explores the CSR practices in a Corporation in accordance with Companies Act, 2013, along with its implementations as required by them.

Lastly, Chapter sixth, of this dissertation deals with the conclusions reached along with the relevant suggestions.

Researcher hopes this dissertation will be helpful in understanding the policies relating to Corporate Social Responsibility with special emphasis on the New Companies Amendment Act of 2013.

Acknowledgements

*DEDICATED TO ALL THOSE PEOPLE
WHO CHANGE THE LIFE OF OTHERS
BY LIVING AS AN EXAMPLE.
AND
BY EMPOWERING OTHERS
FOR GRATENESS.
THANK YOU.*

Table Of Contents

Table Of Statutes / Convention

Statutes:

1. Constitution of India
2. Companies Act, 2013
3. Companies (Corporate Social Responsibility) Rules, 2014
4. Corporate Responsibility for Environmental Protection
5. The Companies Bill, 2009
6. Corporate Social Responsibility Voluntary Guidelines,2010
7. Companies Bill, 2011

Conventions:

1. The UN Guiding Principles on Business and Human Rights
2. ILO's tripartite declaration of principles on multinational enterprises and social policy
3. OECD Guidelines for multinational enterprises
4. United Nations Global Compact

Table Of Cases:

INTRODUCTION

1. __INTRODUCTION__

"The world cannot get out of its present state of catastrophe with the same thinking that got it there in the first place."

--**ALBERT EINSTEIN[1]**.

Industrial Revolution in the early years of the 19th century was one of the major turning points in the history of civilization. Man's ability to make use of resources for improving the lives of fellow men was one of the drivers which led to this revolution. As time went, the industrial output and the multiplicity and intricacy of products increased. This increase has continued and it fills our lives with innumerable objects of desire and luxury, along with the daily human requirements. Along with this revolution, there was a cultural revolution in the way people lived. Industrial units and related activities provided the masses with employment and a means of growth and development. Laws, regulations and policies essential for industrial growth were developed and the world progressed. Over a period of time industries became more and more complex and their influence increased to hitherto unknown realms of research, knowledge and ability. The financial profitability ensured that more and more stakeholders were involved in the functioning of the industrial and financial sectors.

Thereafter, the responsibility of companies towards their shareholders was considered so enormous that there was a time when the use of any corporate funds for philanthropic purposes as well as for illegal practices evolved and after three quarters of a century the U.S. Supreme Court, in 1953, set a precedent by formally affirming the corporation's right to make donations, which was already acceptable to the general society (Sharfman, 1994). This acceptability is evident from the fact that as early as the 1930's and 1940's there are references to social responsibility, including *Chester Barnard's, The Functions of the Executive* in 1938, *J.M. Clark's, Social Control of Business in 1939 and Theodore Krep's, Measurement of the Social Performance of Business in 1940,* and in the poll conducted by *Fortune* magazine of businessmen asking them about their social responsibilities in 1946 (Carroll, 1999)[2]. Thus, social responsibility of business refers to its obligation to take those decisions and perform those actions which are desirable to terms of the objectives and values of our society. The postulation of social responsibilities by business enterprises implies that they respect the aspirations of society and would try their best to contribute to the achievement of these aspirations along with their profit interests. The growing realizations that the capital market, corporations are after all, created by society and must therefore serve the society, indeed merely make profit from it made the corporations responsible and attentive towards societial benefits and escort to the maturity of the concept of the Social Responsibility. Thus, this concept of 'social responsibility' of business enterprises leads to the emergence of the phrase "Corporate Social Responsibility", which is said to be a situations where the firm goes beyond compliance and acts to promote some social good, beyond the interests of the firm and which the society call for. The, World Business Council on Sustainable Development's (WBCSD) use the term Corporate Social Responsibility to define organization's commitment to the society and the environment within which it operates.

Milton Friedman also argues that, "*....few trends could so thoroughly undermine the very foundations of our free society as the acceptance by corporate officials of a social responsibility other than to make as much money for their stockholders as possible.*"[3]

International Organization for Standardization, 2007, said that "....Organizations around the world, as well as their stakeholders, are becoming increasingly aware of the need for socially responsible behaviour"

However, at the end of the 20th century the impact of businesses on society has grown and the range of stakeholder's concerns has fluctuated from narrow view of owners to a broader range of constituent (including employees and customers) and also a disproportionate focus on stakeholder's welfare has gained momentum. Thus, the idea in contrast to the common perception that business exists only for maximizing profits for its owners and it is irrelevant to talk of public good, has somehow becoming a vanishing point. The rules of corporate governance have changed too. And there has been a range of reactions to this change. According to Zennifer Zerk;

"Globalization" is giving rise to a new political struggle, not between states and multinationals or necessarily between

north and south, but between people and Corporations. In the age of globalization, corporations and business enterprises are no longer confined to the traditional boundaries of the nation-state. Therefore, it is said that the problem which the world faces in 21st century, Corporate Social Responsibility is the answer to it.

On the one hand globalization and liberalization have provided a great opportunity for corporations to be internationally competitive by expanding their production-base and market share. On the other hand, the same business poses a great challenge to the sustainability and practicability of such mega-businesses, particularly in the context of the emerging disgruntlement against multinational companies in different parts of the world. Labourers, marginalized consumers, environmental activists and social activists have protested against the exceptional dominance of multinational companies. The explosive development of civil society organizations (CSOs) and non-governmental organizations (NGOs) which often challenge corporate behavior has compelled companies to respond. NGOs at the center of this grassroots Corporate Social Responsibility movement are extremely assorted in terms of goals – ranging from outright attacks on the fundamental power of companies to efforts, to enhance beneficial and reduce detrimental impacts, and equally heterogeneous in terms of strategies deployed – ranging from confrontation to engagement, from stand-alone operations to highly sophisticated coalitions among NGOs.

Further, the on-going revolution in communication technology and the effectiveness of knowledge-based economies has created a new model of business and corporate governance. A growing awareness about the need for ecological sustainability and the New Economy framework, with an unparalleled stress on communication and image merchandising, have cemented the way for a new generation of business leaders concerned about the responses of the community and the sustainability of the environment. Nowadays with the changing market situation this focus is shifting and including three other factors: environmental, educational and health responsibilities. Companies or organizations have started spending their social responsibility money for environmental benefits, public health care initiatives and for providing free education to the wads of employees and underprivileged. There has been a noticeable transition from giving as an obligation or charity to giving as a strategy or responsibility. Today, the situation has become such, that, for the corporates their motive of "maximization of profits" has been replaced by "optimization of profits.

Political pressure has also prompted initiatives in governmental and intergovernmental organizations. Proposals have arisen within *the United Nations (United Nations provides* **"The UN Guiding Principles on Business and Human Rights"**[4] *), the International Labor Organization (ILO)*[5]*, and the OECD*[6]*, the governments of the United Kingdom, France, and the European Union.* Even though it has resisted linking economic and social concerns, the *WTO* has also been a focal point for debate about the scope of business responsibilities since the WTO sets the rules for the global trade. The range of issues is equally diverse – environment, labor rights, human rights, trade, corruption, corporate governance, health, transparency and disclosure, etc. And increasingly, governments of developing nations are weighing in, sometimes in opposition to Corporate Social Responsibility initiatives. Corporations have responded sometimes defensively and sometimes with efforts to demonstrate that voluntary approaches will achieve better results. The another important international initiatives for Corporate Social Responsibility is the *United Nations of Global Compact (UNGC)* which provides a high profile means for mobilizing and encouraging enterprises to integrate CSR into their daily operations[7]

It is in this context that various new initiatives have been taken by the Government of India in regard to develop the mandatory policy on corporate social responsibility. The foremost among them is replacing the 57 years old Companies Act, 1956 and passing of the New Companies Act, 2013 with the inclusion of the Corporate Social Responsibility mandate in it. Therefore, it is an attempt to supplement the government's efforts of equitably delivering the benefits of growth and to engage the Corporate World with the country's development memo.

Thus, Corporate Social Responsibility is viewed as a comprehensive set of policies, practices and programmes that are integrated into business operations, supply claims and decisions making process throughout the company – wherever the company does business – and includes responsibility for current and past actions as well as future impact.

In a nutshell, Corporate Social Responsibility (CSR) is the new buzzword in the modern age, and today, almost all big companies have specific guidelines on Corporate Social Responsibility. The business houses consciously engaged in efforts to give something back to society.

1. <u>**Review of Literature[8]:**</u>

The concept of Corporate Social Responsibility (CSR) has become a significant concept in the study of researchers, scholars and industrialists etc. Similarly, I, also made an effort to review the literature of those scholars, researchers, analysts, industrialists and imminent jurists who are concomitant with Corporate Social Responsibility.

Corporate Social Responsibility concept is not of the recent origin and its paradigm has been traced back to the works of **Mr.Bowen, in 1953,** particularly his book "The*Social Responsibilities of Businessmen*"[9]: CSR denotes to the compulsions of businessmen to chase those strategies, to make those choices, or to follow those lines of action which are required in terms of the goals and values of our society and welfare of mankind.

Mr.Windsor in 2001, in his article scrutinized the impending of Corporate Social Responsibility and its relationship business and society.

Through a speech delivered by Mr. Fredrick, who is the secretary for financial services, based on Corporate Social Responsibility organized by the British consulate in 2004. The utterer reconnoitered the concept of CSR on the basis of survey of 2000 business persons joining the world economic forum in Bevos, in which 7% leaders said that Corporate Social Responsibility is important for the accomplishment of business, while 26% said CSR is of least importance but the shareholder's interest is most important for conducting the businesses affairs. But as per the opinion of the speaker, CSR and corporate governance are harmonizing each other. Corporate governance is a mode of promoting and moving Corporate Social Responsibility among corporations.

Mr.Moon in 2004, in a research paper examined the role of government in accelerating corporate social responsibility among the corporations. The study explained that the teamsters of Corporate Social Responsibility are associated with business and society at large. In conducting business, its reputation, corporation itself, employee's relation knowledge, goals etc are inclusive. Further, the paper cleared that the government is driving force for Corporate Social Responsibility by creating this association true and fair through making policies, rules and regulations in this regard. The research work also boarded others country's position that how their government regulate the businesses for implementing Corporate Social Responsibility.

Mr.Samuel O. Idowu in 2007, in his study of 20 companies in United.Kingdom., submitted that the U.K. companies has now become ethical in the gratification of social responsibility as companies reveal its Corporate Social Responsibility with a view of benefits to the public, and provide information to investors because in their opinion now they are better educated than the previous era.

In the research paper "The standing of Corporate Social Responsibility industry in Australia" Mr.Truscott, Bartlett, Trwoniak in 2009, research based on case study methodology. On the basis of the interview of key persons of industries in Australia, the term Corporate Social Responsibility has been explicated. They stated their views of Corporate Social Responsibility in economic, legal and ethical roles and code of conduct of business and corporations.

In a case study conducted by Mr.Shah, Bhaskar in 2010 on Bharat Petroleum Corporation Ltd. researcher has discussed that there is a broad connection between the corporation and society. Companies have its presence and existence only with the mankind & society. Corporations used the resources of the society. In converse to this, the corporations provide services to the peoples. By the said case study of the BPCL, it was established that corporations has taken a lot of ingenuities in order to render services to the society at large.

Mr. Wharton, stated in his article in 2011 that today, Corporate Social Responsibility has diverse meaning for different corporations. Many of them termed Corporate Social Responsibility in the sense of social issue while other for issues re4lated to the environment. But there are not any obligatory guidelines and policies for Corporate Social Responsibility so that the problem related to the areas of Corporate Social Responsibility can be resolved. More to this, the researcher argued about various views and plans of government and other institutions *like union corporate minister like Mr. Murli Deora, Companies Act 1956, Companies Bill 2008 and 2009, Dhavaludani (CEO of non-governmental organization), FICCI etc.* The researcher also segregates the term Corporate Social Responsibility from the other related terms like Corporate Philanthropy, CSV (creating Share Value) etc. Corporate Social Responsibility has explained in the way the how conduction of business marked its place in the society.

"Corporate Social Responsibility and institutional theory: new perspective on private governance" a study conducted by Mr. Brammer, Jcakson & Matten in 2012 stated that Corporate Social Responsibility is not a charitable task but it is something more to this. This research work stated that Corporate Social Responsibility had well-defined under institutional theory. According to this theory corporate social affairs are not the charitable tasks but it is a part of edge between corporations and society at large. Rules/Regulation/ governance are essential for augmenting the corporate performance of businesses through CSR. This theory also claimed that in what form corporations should take its social accountabilities whether historical, political or in the form of legal compulsion.

"What we know and don't know about corporate social responsibility: A review and research agenda" is the research work conducted by Mr. Agunis, glovas in 2012. This research work gives a context of Corporate Social Responsibility activities which affects outcomes of actions of stake- holder both internally and externally.

Mr. Wharton on 23 may 2012, through an article published by him, signified that according to changing scenario Corporate Social Responsibility importance are also shifting in its nature and context. The researcher propounded that the coming group of business will give unwarranted value to the Corporate Social Responsibility activities while previous researchers *like Milton Friedman* stated that Corporate Social Responsibility is a *window dressing for businesses*. More to this, in this article, with the help of various instances it has discussed that companies indulged in Corporate Social Responsibility are more lucrative in terms of money, capital and other assets. Some researchers and corporations termed Corporate Social Responsibility as *cost saver* while some other stated that it is a reputation building action. So, it may be concluded that CSR is beneficial for the society as well as corporations.

"*Initializing Corporate Social Responsibility*: The top three essential elements" is an article which was published in Triple Bottom Line Magazine presented Corporate Social Responsibility in accordance with the changing time period. It has exposed through this research that Corporate

Social Responsibility should be at the core and the corner of business goals and objectives.

The views of former president Dr. APJ Abdul Kalam was highlighted in Economic Times in 2012, in a Corporate Social Responsibility award function conducted by industry body Assocham. Mr. Kalam submitted that corporations should bestow some part of its goal to corporate services. It should make obligatory for all the corporations to devote a percentage of its profit on CSR. Mr. Kalam also stated about the anticipated bill on corporate spending on Corporate Social Responsibility. As per his views CSR expected greater importance in building the lives of the countrymen.

"Corporate Social Responsibility: A cloak for crooks" is another article published in The Economic Times on 21 Oct. 2012 sightsaw that there are many corporations which have betrothed in Corporate Social Responsibility yet they are suffering from financial crisis , fraud and other unsocial causes. An example has been taken about the company Satyam Computer Services. This corporation has won several awards in the area of Corporate Social Responsibility.

"Corporate Social Responsibility looks set to emerge as an independent stream with measurable output" by *Mr.Bhattacharyya & Chaturvedi in 2012*, stated about the anticipated bill of Corporate Social Responsibility that how it will affect the company's policies and actions. The researchers shared their views and said that due to this bill, the corporations are compelled to invest certain capital for society.

"Is Corporate Social Responsibility all Bullshit?" it is an article presented on India Corporate Social Responsibility depicted that companies are not having strong will power to invest in social activities more to this they are not aware

about the thrust areas which comes under Corporate Social Responsibility. The reason of this problem is ignorance about the concept of Corporate Social Responsibility and not any legal framework. As solution to this problem the researcher stated that knowledge should be provided in the institutions through various training, induction programmes etc. Researcher is also of the opinion that if needed, the foreign experiences should be used in our country for the welfare of the society.

'Corporate Social Responsibility is the face of industry face of doing trade'. This view was stated by Mr. Bibhu Parshed in an article presented in 2012

A news which highlighted the strategy of DELL Co. in the Economic Times (11 Jan.2013) this news said that Dell's for encouraging its employees in priming Corporate Social Responsibility. As per the said news company's employees are the power that compelled the company to do more for the societal benefit. Corporation with its employees has engaged in social responsibility activities in the areas of education, environment and employee's welfare. This news also stated about other corporations like *Maruti and Gogrej* that these corporations also managing to give training to its employees for concocting them for community services. For providing awareness to the employees regarding community problem and their solution Maruti Company is running a program named e-parivartan for a group of employees.

3. <u>OBJECTIVES OF THE RESEARSCH:</u>

- To explore the various definitions and descriptions of Corporate Social Responsibility (CSR).

- To study the evolutionary aspect relating to the development of Corporate Social Responsibility, both globally and in India.
- To elaborate upon the guidelines and policies governing Corporate Social Responsibility, in India.
- To examine the constitutional perspective and judicial accountability on Corporate Social Responsibility in India.
- To study the disposition of current Corporate Social Responsibility practices in India, in light of New Companies (Amendment) Act, 2013.

4. <u>SCOPE OF THE STUDY</u>

Scope of the study is limited to study the concept of Corporate Social Responsibility established in India and mostly focusing on the New Companies (Amendment) Act, 2013.

5. <u>HYPOTHESIS:</u>

The present study determines important key factors of Corporate Social Responsibility for Indian business. The study attempts to understand the general realization and knowledge of practices of the corporate social responsibility in India with reference to new Amendment Act of 2013. My hypothesis is that the new amendment act of 2013 is not sufficiently inclined towards socially responsibility practices and more to this the mandatory provisions as inserted by the new Amendment Act to spend 2% of their average net profit in the previous three years on CSR activities is not adequate and needed intelligible consideration. I am also of the opinion that classification of corporations for the purpose to make them accountable for implementation of CSR is inappropriate and the entire corporation should made liable to implement Corporate Social Responsibility activities irrespective of their annual turnover, net worth or net profit.

6. <u>RESEARCH METHODOLOGY</u>:

The dissertation is an attempt of empirical and exploratory research, based on the secondary data sourced from legal commentaries, journals, magazines, articles and media reports extensively used for the study.

<u>1.7 CHAPTERIZATIONS</u>:

Chapter 1: INTRODUCTION TO CORPORATE SOCIAL RESPONSIBILITY (CSR):

This chapter introduce the term Corporate Social Responsibilities which explain the background of the term along with its changing dimensions after coming of the globalization in the beginning of the 21st century in the world and in India.

CHAPTER 2: History and Evolution of Corporate Social Responsibility

This chapter undergoes the historical and evolutionary aspect of the concept Corporate Social Responsibility in the World as well as in India along with the various phases.

CHAPTER 3: CONCEPT OF CORPORATE SOCIAL RESPONSIBILTY

This chapter deals with the concept of Corporate Social Responsibility along with its meaning, definitions and its importance in today's world.

CHAPTER 4: LEGAL PERSPECTIVE OF CORPORATE SOCIAL RESPONSIBILITY IN INDIA:

This chapter comprises and discusses the legal framework of corporate social responsibility in India along with the available Acts, provisions and committee's framework, with more emphasis to the New Companies (Amendment) Act, 2013.

CHAPTER 5: Role of Judiciary in shaping Corporate Social Responsibility:

This chapter contains the role of judiciary in interpreting and shaping the corporate social responsibility in India.

Suggestions/Recommendations & Conclusion:

In the last chapter the researcher has given an overview of the conclusion arrived and has given suitable suggestions and recommendations.

[1] Soheli Ghose, "A look into Corporate Social Responsibility in Indian and emerging economies" *International Journal of Business and Management Invention ISSN (Online)*

[2] Ajay Gajanan Bhave, Experiences of the Role of Government to promote Corporate Social Responsibility initiatives in the private sector – recommendations to the Indian state of Gujarat, Published in 2006 by IIIEE, Lund University,

[3] Freidman, Milton, "Capitalism and Freedom," University of Chicago Press, 1962, p133.

[4] The UN guiding principles provide assistance to states and businesses to fulfill their existing obligations towards respecting and protecting human rights and fundamental freedoms and comply with the existing laws. These principles act as global standards for addressing the risk of human rights violation related to business activity. In circumstances when these laws are breached or the guidance is not adhered to, suitable remedies have also

been recommended. The primary focus is on the protection of human rights by both, the state and the business enterprises, and the principles broadly outline the manner in which the framework can be implemented.

[5]ILO's **tripartite declaration of principles on multinational enterprises and social policy, it is a** voluntary declaration whose adoption by governments, employers and multinational organizations is encouraged, with the intention of further ensuring labour and social standards. This is particularly for organizations that operate across multiple countries. Focus is on core labour standards such as (i) freedom of association and the right to collective bargaining (prohibition of discrimination, bonded and forced labour) (ii) industrial relations (no trade union restrictions, regular discussions between management and labour, and the provision of a forum to lodge complaints in case of labour standard violation) (iii) employment opportunities (creation of job security, improved living and working conditions and ensuring that wages are on par with those of other enterprises in the same country).

[6]OECD Guidelines for multinational enterprises elaborate on the principles and standards for responsible business conduct for multinational corporations. These guidelines were recently updated in 2011. They cover areas such as employment, human rights, environment, information disclosure, combating bribery, consumer interests, science and technology, competition and taxation. They contain defined standards for socially and environmentally responsible corporate behaviour, and also provide procedures for resolving disputes between corporations and communities or individuals adversely impacted by business activities.

[7] UNGC is world's largest corporate citizenship initiative with the objective to mainstream the adoption of sustainable and socially responsible policies by businesses around the world. The 10 principles of the UN Global Compact have been derived from various UN conventions such as the Universal Declaration of Human Rights, ILO's Declaration on Fundamental Principles and Rights at Work, the Rio Declaration on environment and development, and the UN Convention Against Corruption. These principles cover four broad areas: Human rights (support and respect the protection of international human rights and ensure that business is not complicit with human rights abuses) Labour rights (uphold the freedom of association and effective recognition of the right to collective bargaining, elimination of all forms of forced and compulsory labour, effective abolition of child labour and elimination of description in respect of employment and occupation) Environment (support a precautionary approach to environmental challenges, undertake initiatives to promote greater environmental responsibility and encourage the development of environmental friendly technology) Governance (work against corruption in all forms, including bribery and extortion).

[8] GEETA RANI*; & KALPANA HOODA, CORPORATE SOCIAL RESPONSIBILITY: REVIEW OF LITERATURE, International Journal of Social Science & Interdisciplinary Research_ISSN 2277 3630

IJSSIR, Vol. 2 (6), JUNE (2013)Online available at indianresearchjournals.com

[9] published in 1953 (Valor, 2005)

CHAPTER TWO

CORPORATE SOCIAL RESPONSIBILITY- HISTORY & EVOLUTION:

"Without completing its Social Responsibility, No Business can live".[1]

2.1. Corporate Social Responsibility- Evolution[2]:

Corporate social responsibility is not of the recent origin, just as a corporation's history of causing social and environmental damage dates back to the East India Company. While some corporations have followed opportunist approach to make profit regardless of the impacts on society, benefiting from the slave trade, colonialism and war, but simultaneously there is equally a history of a small minority of companies those who adopted a more philanthropic and humanitarian approach by considering the needs of employees or supporting the poor section of the society. The creation of cooperatives and mutual as alternative forms to the corporation reflects the long- standing concerns around the impacts of corporations.

There has never been a zenith when corporations acted in accordance with the benefit of society. But the unparalleled power of corporations in recent decades, together with an informed and intellectual society, has created a real menace to the legitimacy of the corporation, which CSR seeks to thwart.

"Corporate Social Responsibility" was devised in year **1953** with the work of Bowen's 'Social Responsibility of Businessmen', which putted the question of utmost importance that 'what responsibilities to society can corporations are reasonably predictable to shoulder?' this subject was expanded in year **1960** suggesting that beyond the four walls of legal obligations corporations had certain social responsibilities. In the year **1984**, the imminent management consultant Peter Drucker wrote about the imperious to turn social problems into economic openings.

Throughout the decades of **1970** and **1980** academic platform for discussing of the concept of CSR cultivated, but the first company which originally published a report in this connection was Ben and Jerry's in the year **1989**, and the first corporation in the year **1998** was 'Shell'.

In the late 1970's both the *Organization of Economic Co- operation and Development (OECD)*, and *United Nations Centre on Transnational Corporations (UNCTC)* proceeded with evolving codes of conduct in an effort to regulate the different aspects of globalized corporate sector. In 1976, the OECD, with a alliance of 30 powerful industrialized nations, recognized the snags associated with corporations functioning across borders, they established a set of guidelines and regulations to affluence the workings of globalization; setting the 'rules for the play' for direct investment by other countries, and creating a scenario of sureness and expectedness in overseas companies.

'Guidelines for Multinational Enterprises' by *OCED* shielded areas such as accountancy, payment of taxes, and enforcement and operation in accordance with municipal laws of nations. Aforesaid guidelines are meant at countries rather than corporations, and their compliance can be equally important for attainment of listings in certain stock exchanges and credits for the export.

United Nations Centre on Transnational Corporations (UNCTC) code of conduct was intended to homogenize corporate abuse rather than to facilitate the corporations for access to new emerging markets, and predictably was least efficacious, said code might have been a important instrument for regulating the excess of corporations, but the body was pull to bits under pressure from corporations and amalgamated into the UN Conference on Trade and Development an instrumentality for the promotion of the foreign venture.

The decades of 1970s and 1980s saw major international proscribes of corporations investing in South Africa, Notably Barclays Bank, and Nestlé. This shun over the company's aggressive milk formula marketing strategies in the global South. This period was epitomized by argumentative demonstration that forced change from corporations by confronting the marque.

Earth Summit in Rio in the year 1992 was a significant tick in the fruition of CSR as corporate immersion succeeded in encumbering the Summit's determined effort to 'find a way to standstill the devastation of inimitable resources given by nature and pollution.'

At the time of build-up, offer forwarded by Sweden and Norway for guiding and regulating the multinationals, based on the work of *United Nations Centre on*

Transnational Corporations (UNCTC), were crumpled in favour of environmentalism voluntarily beloit by the corporations.

There was unprecedented level of involvement by the multinational corporations in the summit, with an alliance of corporations 48 in numbers, formed explicitly to stimulus its upshots. This new association, the *Business Council for Sustainable Development BCSD*, subsequently become the *World Business Council on Sustainable Development WBCSD* was established by Stephan Schmidheiny, a Swedish millionaire at the invitation of Maurice Strong, who was chairing the summit. The BCSD along with *International Chamber of Commerce (ICC)* took a pushbike method which efficiently shifted the discussion. On one hand the ICC confronted any measures that moved towards corporate control, and on the other hand BCSD proclaimed the changing course of action of industries towards self-regulation which is voluntary in nature. This type of approach has come to epitomize lobbying of corporations against the reformist ruling of regulation and control.

This anti-corporation repercussion came to its pinnacle in year 1995, as the attention moved on Shell. In this year the corporation stood blamed of connivance in the implementation of Ken Saro Wiwa and 8 other activists in Nigeria, more to this it is also pursued by Greenpeace over the decision to sink the Brent Spar oil platform. Shell momentarily lost the confidence of general public as well as that of investors. By the license to function on the line which approaches to persuade the class that companies played a significant and evocative part in society was essential and capitalism had to be given a model for promotion of Corporate Social Responsibility.

Aftermath, Shell published a statement of business principles demarcating its core values of honesty, integrity and respect for people. The company's policies motivated on the 'magic keys' - 'openness and dialogue', pioneering the practice of producing CSR reports with its 'Profit and Principles - Does there have to be a choice? Report of Shell published in 1998 which was shaped by associates in advertising and recognized by the environmental consultancy Sustainability. The construction of the said report was united with a worldwide advertising campaign concentrating on issues related with the environment and website reassuring the stakeholders to Tell Shell, which was empowering the corporation to appear to comprise the public in its process of decision-making. The approach of corporation was successful in reconstructing the Shell's reputation amongst persons involved in decision making.

So, Corporate Social Responsibility evolved as a straight reaction by companies to anti-corporate crusading and the campaigns for causing the reputational damage. It signifies a success for companies in reviving their image in public and inhabiting the issue which causes the social and environmental impressions on the business of corporations. Mr.Tom Delfgaauw, the former vice president at Shell for sustainable development, labeled the company's problems in the middle of-1990s as 'It is the best thing that ever happened to us, firstly because we have come out of it as the much, much stronger as a corporation, and secondly because it augmented a great many desirable corporate progresses'.

CSR: Rise in the Concept

In the year 1990s Corporate Social Responsibility has become an established notion with major companies such as (PWC) Price Waterhouse Coopers, KPMG and Burson

Marsteller adopted the CSR services in their provisions. New consultancies, such as Sustainability (1989), Business for Social Responsibility (1992) and CSR Europe (1996), also leaped up over this period, and all promising to protect industrial sector from remonstration. Various university research centers and the CSR conferencing circuits have also arisen in the late 1990s. More to this CSR evolved afar from the simple codes of conduct and reporting to include more widespread negotiation with participants, Non-Governmental Organizations activities and 'multi-stakeholder ingenuities' such as the Ethical Trading Initiative (1993) and the Forest Stewardship Council (1998), bringing together corporations, NGOs and in some cases governments also played active role in that.

Subsequent years saw a overabundance of deliberative wits and codes of conduct being developed, by individual corporations as well as sectoral codes and international structures. Codes included the International Organization for Standardization's **ISO14001** in the year 1996, the Global Reporting Initiative Sustainability Reporting Guidelines in the year 1997, Social Accountability International's **SA8000** in the year 1998, Accountability Assurance Standard in the year 1999, and the United Nation's Global Compact in the year 1999.

Most important in this connection is the UN's Global Compact. This Compact was structured by the office of the Kofi Annan, the then Secretary General along with the substantial contribution from the International Chamber of Commerce, which provided the utmost inputs to guarantee a 'Business Friendly' methodology. This Compact is a set of nine ideologies on basic human rights, sustainable environment policies and rights of labour. Recently principle on corruption is also included in this making it 10 in numbers.

Most of the NGOs have been given extremely critical approach to the Compact because as per their opinion it is not having any monitoring or implementation mechanism and it permits the corporations to suitable the name of the United Nations to strengthen their standings without requiring them to change their actions. Deborah Doane, argues in 'Red Tape to Road Signs' that 'By encouraging these implements as substitutes for international governance institutions, the UN and OECD effectively destabilizes the ability of municipal governments to put forward a diverse tactic.'

World Summit on Sustainable Development (WSSD) in year 2002, manifest the capping of Corporate Social Responsibility. Despite the summit delivered much the similar consequence as Rio, with over 280 'new' partnerships between government and industry. Christian Aid has documented the way in which discussion of the issue of corporate regulation in the summit's agenda, changed from working towards a 'multilateral agreement', to simply 'promoting best practices'. But amongst activists and NGOs, there were, disappointment with the CSR model was clear. While many NGOs continue to engage with business, the calls for corporate accountability are growing with campaigns such as International Right to Know Campaign in the USA, the CORE Coalition in the UK and other ingenuities globally persisting for more legally enforceable rather than regulation which is voluntary in nature.

2.2. Corporate Social Responsibility: Evolution in India[3]:

The genesis of corporate social responsibility in our country refers to changes over time of the cultural norms of corporation's rendezvous of corporate social responsibility CSR. ***The conception of*** *Corporate Social Responsibility* ***(CSR) emerged from the*** *'Vedic era'* ***when history was not recorded in our country. During that period, Kings had an onus towards society and public and traders displayed their own business accountability by building places of worship, education, wells, Bathing Ghats etc.***

The history of Corporate Social Responsibility in India has divided into four phases which run equivalent to India's historical development and has consequently resulted in different slants towards CSR. However none of the phases are inert and the features of each phase are having a kind of overlapping with each other.

The First Phase

During the first phase main drivers of Corporate Social Responsibility are the charity and generosity were the. Culture, religion, family values and tradition and industrialization had a persuasive effect on CSR. During the pre-industrialization era, which persisted till 1850, well-heeled merchants shared a part of their wealth with the wider society by way of setting up temples for a religious cause bathing ghats, wells etc. Moreover, these merchants helped the society in getting over phases of famine and epidemics by fulfilling the basic needs of food from their godowns and money and thus fortifying a vital position in the general public. After the emergence of colonial rule in India from 1850s onwards, the tactic towards Corporate Social Responsibility transformed. The entrepreneur families of the 19th century such as Tata, Godrej, Bajaj, Modi, Birla, Singhania were strongly motivated towards economic as well as social deliberations. But it has been perceived that their determinations towards social as well as industrial development were not only obsessed by selfless and religious motives but also influenced by attaining their political objectives and influenced by class wise classification which was not just and appropriate.

The Second Phase

During the second phase, at the time of independence movement in our country, there was increased pressure on Indian Businesspersons to reveal their commitment towards the progress of the society at large. This was when Mahatma Gandhi introduced the conception of "trusteeship", according to which the business persons had to accomplish their wealth so as to benefit the common man or every single individual of our country. According to him-"I desire to end capitalism almost, if not quite, as much as the most advanced socialist. But our methods differ. My theory of trusteeship is no make-shift, certainly no camouflage. I am confident that it will survive all other theories." These word of Mahatma Gandhi acme his argument towards the concept of "trusteeship". Gandhi's inspiration put compression on various entrepreneurs to act in a manner towards building the nation and its complete social-economic and political growth. According to Gandhi, Our corporations were supposed to be the "temples of modern India". Due to his influence businesses established various trusts for education and also helped in setting up scientific institutions & training programmes. Functions of these trusts were largely in line with reforms which pursued to abolish untouchability, hearten empowerment of women and development of rural class and weaker section of the society.

The Third Phase- (1960-1980)

Third phase of Corporate Social Responsibility (1960–80) had its connections to the constituent of "mixed economy", appearance of Public Sector Undertakings

(PSUs) and laws relating to set standards for labour and environmental issues. In this phase the private sector was compelled to take a backbench. Public sector was appreciated as the chief driving force of development. Because of the rigorous laws, rules and regulations contiguous the activities of the private sector, this phase was described as an "era of command and control". Policy of providing industrial licensing, high taxes and restraints on the private sector led this phase to the corporate derelictions. This led our country to enact the legislation regarding corporate governance, and various labour and environmental conflicts involved therein. PSUs were established by the state to guarantee proper and bonafide distribution of resources to the needy section of the society. But the public sector was effective only to a certain limited extent. This led to shift of expectation from the public to the private sector and their active involvement in the socio-economic development of the country became unconditionally necessities. In the year 1965 academicians, politicians and businessmen of our country set up a national workshop on Corporate Social Responsibility which aimed at understanding. All of them emphasized upon transparency, social accountability and regular stakeholder dialogues in Indian corporate sector but despite of such efforts made by the then ruling authorities the Corporate Social Responsibility failed to no-win situation mist.

The Fourth Phase- 1980 onwards

During fourth phase started from 1980 our companies started deserting from their outmoded rendezvous with Corporate Social Responsibility and combined it into a sustainable business policy. During 1990s the first launch towards globalization and economic liberalization were undertaken forward. Regulation and accrediting mechanism were partly done away, which gave a enhancement to the economy the symbols of which are very palpable today. Augmented growth of the economy helped our corporations to grow rapidly and it made them more eager and able to aid towards social problems. Globalization has transmuted our country into an important terminus in terms of manufacturing of TNCs are concerned. Markets are becoming more and more concerned to improve the standards of labours and environment in the developing countries; Indian corporations dealing in the international markets need to be vigilant for compliance of the international criterions.

However, the scene of Corporate Social Responsibility in India changed with the introduction of New Companies (Amendment) Act 2013. The industrial foyers are humming with the Corporate Social Responsibility clause introduced by the new Companies Act 2013. Thus, the India becomes the first country to have a mandatory provision of corporate social responsibility for establishing the concept of welfare state in true sense of terms.

2.3. Conclusion:

Thus from the aforesaid discussion it is concluded that now a days the gage of measurement or evaluations of business is not like that as it was used to be about fifty years ago or pre independence. At that time only that business organizations was considered good which was earning profit for its owner but today situations is absolutely changed. Today the responsibility of the business is not limited to its owner but it has assumed large dimensions. Business has to look towards the interests of many other parties along with the interests of the owner. The employees, consumers, suppliers, competitors, governments, community and even the world happen to be the other parties. Today only that business is considered good which keep in minds the interest of these parties along with the interests of the owner. This responsibility of the business, which includes the satisfactions of these parties along with the owner, is called the corporate social responsibility of the business which has gain a lot of importance throughout the world. Various initiatives have been taken internationally and nationally for the implementations of the CSR policies. However, India becomes the first country to have a mandatory CSR provisions through the newly amended Companies Act, which came to be known as Companies Act, 2013.

[1] NCERT, *Business Studies for Class XI*, 143-144, (8th Edition Revised)

[2]http://www.corporatewatch.org.uk/?lid=2682, the evolution of CSR

[3] HUCHHE GOWDA, THE EVOLUTION OF CORPORATE SOCIAL

RESPONSIBILITY (CSR) IN INDIA, Indian Streams Research Journal ISSN:-2230-7850 Volume 3, Issue. Available online at www.isrj.net5, June. 2013

CHAPTER THREE

CONCEPT OF CORPORATE SOCIAL RESPONSIBILITY

3.1. Meaning of the term Corporate Social Responsibility:

"Every large company should be thought of as a social venture; that is an unit whose existence and decision can be justified in so far as they serve for the public or social purposes" Dahl.

The functions of corporations by and large have been implicit in terms of a commercial business example of thoughts that focuses purely on financial parameters of achievement. Companies have been regarded as entity that gratify to the demand of market by giving goods and services, onus lies on the corporations for establishing affluence and job oppurtunities, market position of the corporations has customarily been an act of monetary recital and making profit. But it has been observed over the past decades that, as a result of emergence of globalization and vital environmental issues, the sensitivity of the role of companies in the broader community context within which it is operative, have been changed. Stakeholders at present are reconsidering the funnctions of corporations by taking into consideration the expanded responsibility of the corporations towards the general public and environment, ahead of their economic activities, and are evaluating that whether they are performing their functions in an principled and socially responsible manner or not. Due to the result of this move from "merely financial to economic with an additional social aspect", many forums, institutions and corporations are endorsing the term Corporate Social Responsibility (CSR).

(CSR) Corporate Social Responsibility is explained as a widespread set of rules, regulations, policies, practices and programs which are included by the corporations into their conduction of business, operations, supply chains, and processes of decision making all through the association. Whenever the corporation commenced business the responsibility for present and past actions as well as future impacts were always inclusive in that[1].

Corporate Social Responsibility termed as the responsibility of the corporations to safeguard and augment the norms and values held by the general public within which it conducted its business affairs.

(CSR) Corporate Social Responsibility concerned with a broad series of thoughts, line of action, methodologies and a vast assortment of empirical study. In present scenario, the notion of Corporate Social Responsibility has received eminence to the level that now it is considered as omnipresent, both in the trendy media and also amongst the academicians from various areas & disciplines. It is also mentioned as the corporate conscience, social performance, or sustainable responsible affairs of enterprenures. It is not only depicted in the business sector, but ominipresent in the areas like governmental organisations, public sector, private sector, MNCs, NGOs, and also in the intergovernmental organizations such as the *United Nations Organisation, World Bank or International Labor Organization (ILO).* Taking into consideration on local level the notion of (CSR) Corporate Social Responsibility is directly connected with the relationship between a company and the local community in the local area of which it resides or conducted its business. So, we can say that this term, "corporate social responsibility" is of the great importance and it is used to enclose both social as well as the environmental concerns. More to this after the enactment of mandatory compliance of CSR policies its area is expanded to the fulliest extent.

3.2. DEFINITIONS:

3.2.1. Traditional approach:

The hestogenesis of the (CSR) Corporate Social Responsibility put up has been traced back to the words of **Bowen, 1953,** mentioned his book titles as **"*Social Responsibilities of Businessmen*"**[3]. In which he stated that the 'Corporate Social Responsibility (CSR) refers to the obligations of enterprenures to follow those policies, and to make those decisions, or to follow those lines of action which are advantageous in terms of the objectives and standards of our social order.

Frederick (1960)[4] is of the opinion that: Social responsibility in the conclusive analysis implies a public bearing toward society's economic and human resources and a willingness to see that those resources are used for broad social ends and not simply for the narrowly circumscribed interests of private persons and firms.

Friedman (1962)[5]: There is one and only one social responsibility of business – to use its resources and engage in activities designed to increase its profits so long as it stays within the rules of the game, which is to say, engages in open and free competition without deception or fraud.

In the year **1966, Mr. Davis and Mr. Blomstrom** defined (CSR) as; "It refers to a person's responsibility to judge the effects of his actions and deccisions on the entire social structure. Corporations affect corporate social responsibility when they are in the position of considering the requirements and interest of other section that may be affected by actions of the corporations. While acting in the manner, they appear beyond their firm's pitty financial and technological benefits[6]".

Mr. **Walton in year (1967),** a leading scholar on this connection, in his series of lectures entitled *Corporate Social Responsibilities,* define CSR as;

"It is the intimacy of the relations between the companies and the public" and it was experienced that such associations must be taken into consideration by top management of corporation and the related groups follow their individual goals"[7]

Mr.Backman in year (1975) has defined CSR by giving some examples: Employment of minority section, lessening pollution, active participation in programs to enhance the group of people, better medical care, implementation of best industrial health and safety measures, and various other initiatives intended to improve the quality of life are enclosed by the wide shade of CSR.[8].

Mr. Sethi in year (1975) defined CSR as "It implies bringing activities of corporations up to a height where it is in agreement with the existing social norms, values, and prospect of its implementation.[9]

In the year 1979 Mr. Carroll states that; "CSR of a corporation encompass the monetary, legal, principled, and optional outlook that society has of organizations at a definite point"[10].

Mr. Carroll in the year (1991) depicted his Corporate Social Responsibility model as a pyramid, as shown in **Figure3**. He used his chronological explanation for the relative weighting, and stated that: "All these types of obiligations have always existed to some extent, but in the recent years that principled and philanthropic functions have got an important situate"[11]

Mr.Frederick in the year 1986, recognized corporate social responsibility as "an examination of corporations and a compulsion to work for social upliftment"[13]. He termed it as the (CSR 1) He further said that CSR means that a company should be held answerable for any of its act that affect society, community and the ecology because the social obligations of corporations also arise from two major features of modern organizations: (1) The necessary functions it performs for society; and (2) The vast influence it has on people's lives. According to Mr. Frederick in year 1994, the move to "corporate social responsibility" started from 1970, which he called (CSR 2) and has been defined as corporate social responsiveness as "the capacity of a company to react to social pressure and argue that the bang of the move from CSR 1 to CSR2 is reflected from a theoretical move toward one that focuses on executive accomplishment.[14]

3.2.2. Modern Approach:

In the **1990s John Elkington** developed the **Triple Bottom Line (TBL) also known as thePeople, Planet, Profit (3P's)** formulation. In this model Elkington adds people and planet to the traditional profit bottom line. People stand for the social performances of a firm. Planet for the environmental performances of a firm.

Frederick W, Post J, Davis KE[15]:" Corporate social responsibility can be defined as a principle stating that corporations should be accountable for the effects of any of their actions on their community and environment".

Khoury G, Rostami J, Turnbull JP[16]: "Corporate social responsibility is the overall relationship of the corporation with all of its stakeholders. These include customers, employees, communities, owners/investors, government, suppliers and competitors. Elements of social responsibility include investment in community outreach, employee relations, creation and maintenance of employment, environmental stewardship and financial performance".

Hopkins,   1998[17]define: "Corporate   social responsibility is concerned with treating the stakeholders of the firm ethically or in a socially responsible manner. Stakeholders exist both within a firm and outside. Consequently, behaving socially responsibly will increase the human development of stakeholders both within and outside the corporation".

World Business Council for Sustainable Development (1999)[18] defines Corporate Social Responsibility (CSR) as "The continuing commitment by business to behave ethically and contribute to economic development while improving the quality of life of the workforce and their families as well as of the local community and society at large."

The European Commission's define of CSR[19] as "the responsibility of enterprises for their impacts on society". To completely meet their social responsibility, enterprises "should have in place a process to integrate social, environmental, ethical human rights and consumer concerns into their business operations and core strategy in close collaboration with their stakeholders"

McWilliams and Siegel[20]: "CSR are actions that appear to further some social good, beyond the interests of the firm and that which is required by law".

Organization for Economic Co-operation and Development (OECD) (2003)[21]: Corporate Responsibility involves the 'fit' businesses develop with the societies in which they operate. [...] The function of business in society is to yield adequate returns to owners of capital by identifying and developing promising investment opportunities and, in the process, to provide jobs and to produce goods and services that consumers want to buy. However, corporate responsibility goes beyond this core function. Businesses are expected to obey the various laws which are applicable to them and often have to respond to societal expectations that are not written down as formal law.

Amnesty International – Business Group (UK) (2002)[22] : Companies [have] to recognise that their ability to continue to provide goods and services and to create financial wealth will depend on their acceptability to an international society which increasingly regards protection of human rights as a condition of the corporate license to operate.

The Corporate Responsibility Coalition (CORE) (2003)[23]: As an 'organ of society', companies have a responsibility to safeguard human rights within their direct sphere of operations as well as within their wider spheres of influence.

Global Corporate Social Responsibility Policies Project, 2003[24]define: "Global corporate social responsibility can be defined as business practices based on ethical values and respect for workers, Social communities and the environment".

Business for Social Responsibility, 2003b[25]: "Corporate social responsibility is achieving commercial success in ways that honor ethical values and respect people, communities and the natural environment".

Philip Kotler and Nancy Lee (2005)[26] define CSR as "a commitment to improve community well-being through discretionary business practices and contributions of corporate resources"

Whereas, Mallen Baker refers to CSR[27] as "a way companies manage the business processes to produce an overall positive impact on society."

Kotler, P. and Lee, N.[28]: "CSR is a commitment to improve community well-being through discretionary business practices and contributions of corporate resources".

According to the UNIDO[29], "Corporate social responsibility is a management concept whereby companies integrate social and environmental concerns in their business operations and interactions with their stakeholders. CSR is generally understood as being the way through which a company achieves a balance of economic, environmental and social imperatives (Triple-Bottom-Line Approach), while at the same time addressing the expectations of shareholders and stakeholders. In this sense it is important to draw a distinction between CSR, which can be a strategic business management concept, and charity, sponsorships or philanthropy. Even though the latter can also make a valuable contribution to poverty reduction, will directly enhance the reputation of a company and strengthen its brand, the concept of CSR clearly goes beyond that."

"CSR means managing our business responsibly and sensitively for long-term success. Our goal is not, and never has been, profit at any cost because we know that tomorrow's success depends

on the trust we build today."

The idea behind CSR is that business should accept that it plays more than just an economic role. This means a certain enthusiasm to take more than a liability for the activities and impact in business, but in addition, also take responsibility for their impact on society and the environment (Robins, 2008).

Businesses for themselves, therefore, assume a wide range of socially responsible activities, such an orientation to a large number of activities, trying to affect social and environmental problems. But it also raises wave of criticism. Many professionals and managers, states that such kind of socially responsible activities, which apparently includes every social problem, is not beneficial for either business or the company itself[30]

From the above definitions, it is clear that:

The CSR approach is holistic and integrated with the core business strategy for addressing social and environmental impacts of businesses.

CSR needs to address the well-being of all stakeholders and not just the company's shareholders. Philanthropic activities are only a part of CSR, which otherwise constitutes a much larger set of activities entailing strategic business benefits.

3.3.Essential Elements of Corporate Social Responsibility[31]:

The Corporate Social Responsibility Policy should normally cover following core elements:

1. Care for all Stakeholders:

The companies should respect the interests of, and be responsive towards all stakeholders, including shareholders, employees, customers, suppliers, project affected people, society at large etc. and create value for all of them. They should develop mechanism to actively engage with all stakeholders, inform them of inherent risks and mitigate them where they occur.

2. Ethical working:

Their governance systems should be underpinned by Ethics, Transparency and Accountability. They should not engage in business practices that are abusive, unfair, corrupt or anti-competitive.

3. Respect for the rights and welfare of a workers:

Companies should provide a workplace environment that is safe, hygienic and humane and which upholds the dignity of employees. They should provide all employees with access to training and development of necessary skills for career advancement, on an equal and non-discriminatory basis. They should uphold the freedom of association and the effective recognition of the right to collective bargaining of labour, have an effective grievance redressal system, should not employ child or forced labour and provide and maintain equality of opportunities without any discrimination on any grounds in recruitment and during employment.

4. Admiration for Human Rights:

Companies should respect human rights for all and avoid complicity with human rights abuses by them or by third party[32].

5. Respect for Environment:

Companies should take measures to check and prevent pollution; recycle, manage and reduce waste, should manage natural resources in a sustainable manner and ensure optimal use of resources like land and water, should proactively respond to the challenges of climate change by adopting cleaner production methods, promoting efficient use of energy and environment friendly technologies.

6. Activities for Social and Inclusive Development:

Depending upon their core competency and business interest, companies should undertake activities for economic and social development of communities and geographical areas, particularly in the vicinity of their operations. These could include: education, skill building for livelihood of people, health, cultural and social welfare etc., particularly targeting at disadvantaged sections of society.

3.4. IMPORTANCE OF CORPORATE SOCIAL RESPONSIBILITY[33]:

Corporate Social Responsibility is an important business strategy because, wherever possible, consumers want to buy products from companies they trust; suppliers want to form business partnerships with companies they can rely on; employees want to work for companies they respect; and NGOs, increasingly, want to work together with companies seeking feasible solutions and innovations in areas of common concern. Satisfying each of these stakeholder groups allows companies to maximize their commitment to another important stakeholder group—their investors, who benefit most when the needs of these other stakeholder groups are being met

Corporate Social Responsibility is increasingly crucial to maintaining success in business not only by providing a corporate strategy around which the company can rally, but also by giving meaning and direction to day- to- day operations. Corporate Social Responsibility as an element of strategy is becoming increasingly important for businesses today because of four identifiable trends – trends that seem likely to continue and grow in importance throughout the 21st century:

a. **Growing affluence :**

Affluent consumers can afford to choose the products they buy and are more likely to pay a premium for brand they trust. A poorer society, in need of work and inward investment, is less likely to ensure strict regulations and penalize organizations that might otherwise take their business and money elsewhere. Thus, increasing affluence on a global basis will make corporate social responsibility matter more in future.

a. **Changing Social Expectations:**

Consumers and society in general expect more from the companies whose products they buy. This sense has increased in the light of recent corporate scandals, which reduced public trust of corporations, and reduced public confidence in the ability of regulatory agencies and organizations to control corporate excess.

c. **Globalization and the Free Flow of Information:**

The growing influence of the media conglomerates makes sure that any CSR lapses by companies are brought immediately to the attention of the public – often instantaneously - worldwide. In addition, the Internet fuels communication among like-minded groups and consumers—empowering them to spread their message, while giving them the means to co-ordinate collective action (i.e. a product boycott).

d. **Ecological Sustainability:**

Today, climatic changes, increasing raw materials prices, rising mutation rates among amphibian populations, and other growing evidence shows that the Earth has ecological limits. However, firms that are seen as indifferent to their environmental responsibilities are likely to be criticized and penalized: by court – imposed fines (Exxon Valdez[34]), negative publicity (Monsanto's genetically modified foods[35]), or confrontations by activist group (Friends of the Earth[36]).

3.5. Conclusion:

Business houses all over the world are increasing in realizing their venture in the society and engaging in various social and environmental activities. Corporate Social Responsibility holds a very important place in the development scenario of the world today and can pose as an alternative tool for sustainable development. As companies have shown great concerns for their immediate community and the stakeholders, it can be safely concluded that much of the fate of society lies in the hands of the corporate. A successfully implemented Corporate Social Responsibility strategy calls for aligning these initiatives with business objectives and corporate responsibility across the business principles to make Corporate Social Responsibility sharper, smarter, and focused on what really matters.

Corporate Social Responsibility has a significant role in controlling the perils of uncontrolled development, satisfying the needs of the present generation and at the same time ensuring that the resources of future generations is not jeopardized.

Thus, Corporate Social Responsibility typically includes issues related to business ethics, community engagement, global warming, water management, mange the use of natural resources, human rights etc. So, in order to get sustainable development and to survive in this competitive world, the organizations need to demonstrate a close and good relationship with society.

[1] "Issue Brief: Overview of Corporate Social Responsibility". Business for Social Responsibility Website. Available at: http://www.bsr.org/CSRResources/IssueBriefDetail.cfm?DocumentID=48809

[2] http://www.bombaychamber.com/image002.jpg

[3] published in 1953 (Valor, 2005)

[4] Kakabadse, N.K. Rozuel, C. and Lee-Davies, L. (2005) 'Corporate social responsibility and stakeholder approach: a conceptual review', *Int. J. Business Governance and Ethics*, Vol. 1, No. 4, pp.277–302.,

[5] Kakabadse, N.K. Rozuel, C. and Lee-Davies, L. (2005) 'Corporate social responsibility and stakeholder approach: a conceptual review', *Int. J. Business Governance and Ethics*, Vol. 1, No. 4, pp.277–302.,

[6] Social responsibility of Businessmen (P.12)

[7] (As cited in Carroll, 1999).

[8] (As cited in Carroll, 1999)

[9]Kakabadse, N.K. Rozuel, C. and Lee-Davies, L. (2005) 'Corporate social responsibility and stakeholder approach: a conceptual review', *Int. J. Business Governance and Ethics*, Vol. 1, No. 4, pp.277–302.,

[10] Archie B. Carroll," A Three-Dimensional Conceptual Model of Corporate Performance," Academy of Management Review, 1979,

[11]. Archie B. Carroll, "The Pyramid of Corporate Social Responsibility: Towards the Moral Management of Organizational Stakeholders", Business Horizons, July-August, 1991, p40. (www.sciencetarget.com).

[12] Ibid.

[13] Frederick et al. (1992, p. 30)

[14] (As cited in Samy et al, 2010)

[15] Frederick W, Post J, Davis KE.1992. Business and Society. Corporate Strategy, Public Policy, Ethics, 7th edn. McGraw-Hill: London.

[16] Khoury G, Rostami J, Turnbull JP. 1999. Corporate Social Responsibility: Turning Words into Action. Conference Board of Canada:Ottawa.

[17] Hopkins M.1998. The Planetary Bargain: Corporate Social Responsibility Comes of Age. Macmillan: London.

[18] World Business Council for Sustainable Development. 1999. Corporate Social Responsibility: Meeting Changing Expectations.World Business Council for Sustainable Development: Geneva

[19]http://ec.europa.eu/enterprise/policies/sustainable-business/corporate-social responsibility/index_en.htm

[20] McWilliams, A. and Siegel, D. (2001), "Corporate responsibility: a theory of the firm perspective", The Academy of Management Review, Vol. 26, No. 1, pp. 117–127.

[21] Kakabadse, N.K. Rozuel, C. and Lee-Davies, L. (2005) 'Corporate social responsibility and stakeholder approach: a conceptual review', Int. J. Business Governance and Ethics, Vol. 1, No. 4, pp.277–302.

[22] Kakabadse, N.K. Rozuel, C. and Lee-Davies, L. (2005) 'Corporate social responsibility and stakeholder approach: a conceptual review', Int. J. Business Governance

and Ethics, Vol. 1, No. 4, pp.277–302.

[23] Kakabadse, N.K. Rozuel, C. and Lee-Davies, L. (2005) 'Corporate social responsibility and stakeholder approach: a conceptual review', *Int. J. Business Governance and Ethics*, Vol. 1, No. 4, pp.277–302.

[24] Global Corporate Social Responsibility Policies Project. 2003. A Role for the Government – Issues at Hand, Kenan-Flagler Business School of the University of North Carolina,ChapelHill.http://www.csrpolicies.org/ CSRRoleGov/CSR_Issue/csr_issue.html [20 May 2003].

[25] Business for Social Responsibility. 2003b. Overview of Corporate Social Responsibility. http://www.bsr.org/BSRResources/ IssueBriefDetail.cfm?DocumentID=48809 [23 June 2003].

[26]Corporate Social Responsibility Towards Sustainable Future, A White Paper KPMG IN INDIA

[27]Ibid, Philip Kotler and Nancy Lee, Corporate Social Responsibility : Doing the most Good for Your Company, John Wiley and Sons, Inc. New Jersey, 2005.

[28] Kotler, P. and Lee, N. (2005), Corporate Responsibility: Doing the Most Good for Your Company and Your Cause, Wiley, Hoboken, New Jersey.

[29] http://www.unido.org/what-we-do/trade/csr/ what-is-csr.html#pp1[g1]/0/

[30] Levitt, 1958; Friedman, 1970; Lantos, 2001; Drucker, 2001; Porter and Kramer, 2006; Meehan et al., 2006. (Bhattacharyya, 2008). Willam B. Werther, JR.& David Chandler, University of Maimi, ' Strategic Corporate Social Responsibility, Stakeholders in global environment,pp10-11.

[31] The Challenges of Social Corporate Social Responsibility: Facts for You, May 2013, pp. 38-39 . India,

Ministry of Corporate Affairs, Corporate Social Responsibility Voluntary Guidelines 2009.

[32] The Challenges of Social Corporate Social Responsibility: Facts for You, May 2013, pp. 38-39. India, Ministry of Corporate Affairs, Corporate Social Responsibility Voluntary Guidelines 2009.

[33]*A Guide to Corporate Social Responsibility (CSR)*

[34]http://response.restoration.noaa.gov/photos/exxon.html

[35]http://www.organicconsumers.org/corp/monprotest.cfm

[36] Campaigns: Corporates, http://www.foe.co.uk/campaigns/corporates/index.html

CHAPTER FOUR

LEGAL PERSPECTIVE OF Corporate social RESPONSIBILITY IN INDIA

4.1. CONSTITUTION OF INDIA AND CORPORATE SOCIAL RESPONSIBILITY:

"Corporations are not responsible for all the world's problems, nor do they have the resources to solve them all...but, a well-run company can have a greater impact on social good than any other institution or philanthropic organization."[1]

The Constitution of India under part IV which deals with the Directive Principle of State Policy, commands the 'state' to '**strive to promote the welfare of the people by securing and protecting as effectively as it may a social order in which justice, social, economic and political, shall inform all the institutions of the national life'**. State is unambiguously asked to '**minimize the inequalities in income, and endeavour to eliminate inequalities in status, facilities and opportunities not only amongst** individuals but also amongst groups of people residing in different areas or engaged in different vocations.'[2] Similarly, Constitution also highlights that 'the citizens, men and women equally, have the right to an adequate means of livelihood'[3], 'the ownership and control of the material resources of the community are so distributed as best to subserve the common good'[4], and finally it upholds that 'the operation of the economic system does not result in the concentration of wealth and means of production to the common detriment'[5]Thus, State has been asked that 'it shall, within the limits of its economic capacity and development, make effective provision for securing the right to work, to education and to public assistance in cases of unemployment, old age, sickness and disablement, and in other cases of undeserved want'[6].

Further an Article 48-A was inserted in the part IV of the Constitution of India by 42nd Amendment to the Constitution which for the first time provides a mandate *for the protection of environment and natural resources.*

Thus, Article 48-A prescribe that "the State shall endeavour to protect and improve the environment and to safeguard the forests and wildlife of the country".

Distant from these state duties, the *Constitution of India* delivers adequate duties for the citizens also. Thus, by an amendment to the constitution, Article 51A was inserted in the Part IV, and in so doing Fundamental Duties were casted on citizens.[7] The amendment has an indirect mention to corporate social responsibility where it stress a duty on every citizen "to protect and improve the natural environment including forests, lakes, rivers and wild life, and to have compassion for living creatures,'[8] 'to develop the scientific temper, humanism and the spirit of inquiry and reform',[9] and finally 'to strive towards excellence in all spheres of individual and collective activity so that the nation constantly rises to higher levels of endeavor and achievement.'[10].

Thus, in the case of **State Trading Company. vs. CTO[11] Supreme Court upheld that**

These liberties and protections are assured to 'natural' and 'non-natural' persons equally[12]

In *National Textiles Workers' Union etc.* vs. *P.R. Ram Krishnan,*[13]the constitutional majority held that the socio-economic objectives set down in the directive principles of the Constitution should guide and shape the new corporate philosophy. The management of a private company should show profound concern for the workers. The socio-economic justice will inform all the institutions of textiles in the nation to promote fraternity and dignity of the individuals.

Similarly, the Supreme court in *Consumer Education & Research Centre* vs. *Union of India*[14] held that 'right' of the management in asbestos industry to carry on its business is subject to their obligation to 'protect health of the workmen', 'preserve pollution free atmosphere', and to 'provide safe and healthy conditions of the workmen'. Making an emphatic declaration about role and position of Directive Principles for State Policy,

Further, the apex court in *LIC of India* vs. *Consumer Education and Research Centre Another,*[15] has stated that:

The authorities or a private persons or industry are bound by the principles contained in the development for socio-economic justice of which Social security is a facet of socio-economic justice to the people and a means to livelihood.

In *Dwarkadas Marfatia & Sons* vs. *Board of Trustees of the Port of Bombay*[16], it was held that the Corporation must act in accordance with certain constitutional conscience, and whether they have so acted must be discernible from the conduct of such Corporations.

Likewise, in **Kumari Shrilekha Vidyarthi vs. State of U.P.**[17] Supreme Court has pierced out that the private parties are worried only with their personal interest but the public authorities are expected to act for public good and in public interest. The impact of every action is also on public interest. It imposes public law obligation and impress with that character, the contracts made by the 'state', or its instrumentality. In fact, court tried to find out 'impact analysis' to define and limit the liabilities of state instrumentalities in public domain.

In **Sterling Computers Ltd. vs. M & N Publications Ltd**[18] it was held that even in commercial contracts where there is a public element, it is necessary that relevant considerations are taken into account and the irrelevant consideration discarded.

In **Bears Cave Estate vs. The Presiding Officer**[19]the Madras High Court had made a direct comment that 'the principles behind suffering a person with disabilities are that providing equal opportunities cannot be left only for the mercy by the Government in relation to its servants alone. It is high time the principles behind the Disabilities Act, 1955 must be extended in relation to private employments also and it must be made as part of Corporate Social responsibility of every employee'.

4.2. Emergence of Corporate Social Responsibility guidelines and Companies Act 2013:

The Corporate Social Responsibility scenery in India has undergone immense revolution and renovations in the era of liberalization, privatization and globalization and the modern economic reform and the scope for its improvement in this field continues to exist and can still be worked upon. Various committees, report and guidelines have been issued by the government for the implementations of CSR activities either voluntary or mandatory. Committees called Sachar Committee in 1978 indirectly put weight on CSR activities and lay out that the companies should not ignore their social responsibility and publish social accounts in annual accounts. The acceptance of concept of "social responsibility" must be replicated in the information and disclosure that the companies make available for the benefit of the shareholders, creditors, workers and community. It was recommended that as far as possible social report must be cast both in quantity and monetary terms. The committee also felt the need that the board should also report on the future plans of the company which it has made, in order to discharge its social responsibility and duties.

In April 1998, the Confederation of Indian Industry (CII) came up with, conceivably the first voluntary guideline for corporate governance in the form of ***"Desirable Corporate Governance: A Code."***

, The Ministry of Corporate Affairs also established *a National Foundation for Corporate Governance (NFCG).* It was a result of partnership with the *Confederation of Indian Industry (CII), the Institute of Company Secretaries of India (ICSI) and the Institute of Chartered Accountants of India (ICAI).* The purpose of the NFCG is to promote better corporate governance practices and raise the standard of corporate governance in India towards achieving stability and sustained growth.

In the year 2003, Corporate Responsibility for Environmental Protection (CREP) was introduced by the Indian government as a *guideline for 17 polluting industrial sectors.* There was however no real pressure for implementation or internalization. Thus, the said policy is voluntary in nature.

Later, an official notification by the Government has been released in the form of *'Guidelines' – some mandatory, some voluntary.* [20]The first indication of an official notification on *Corporate Social Responsibility guidelines* was issued by the Ministry of Petroleum and Natural Gas, *whereby public sector oil companies had agreed to spend at least 2% of their net profits on CSR initiatives.* This was followed by a notification titled *'Corporate Social Responsibility Voluntary Guidelines'*, which was issued in December 2009 by the Ministry of Corporate Affairs.[21] However, this guideline contains special provision for corporate social responsibility as it clearly specifies that ***"There was no mention in the earlier Companies Act about corporate social responsibility. We are just mentioning that there will be a Corporate Social Responsibility Policy in each and every company beyond a certain limit, which are profitable companies and which are of certain size"*** Further guidelines were issued for Central Public Sector Enterprises (CPSEs) in April 2010, whereby the creation of a ***'CSR Budget' was made mandatory.***[22]

Thereafter, the Companies Bill, 2009 was introduced in the Lok Sabha, on 3 August 2009. The said Bill of 2009 was brought up to the Parliamentary Standing Committee on Finance, which submitted its report on 31 August 2010 and was withdrawn after the introduction of the Companies Bill, 2011 which was also considered by the Parliamentary Standing Committee on Finance that submitted its report on 26 June 2012. Consequently, the Bill was considered and approved by the Lok Sabha on 18 December 2012 as the Companies Bill, 2012 and then considered and approved by the Rajya Sabha on 8 August 2013. Thus, it received the President's assent on 29 August 2013 and has now become the Companies Act, 2013.

The Companies Act, 2013 makes an effort to introduce the ethos of corporate social responsibility (CSR) in Indian corporates by requiring companies to articulate a corporate social responsibility policy and at least incur a prescribed minimum expenditure on social activities. Thus, the Act of 2013 will set the tone for a more modern legislation which enables growth and greater parameter of the corporate sector in India.

4.2.1. New Companies (Amendment) Act, 2013[23] The Companies Act, 2013 ('2013 Act'), enacted on 29 August 2013 on accord

The Companies (Amendment) Act 2013, enacted on 29 August 2013, has the prospective to be historic momentous, as it aims to corporate governance, simplify regulations, enhance the interest of minority investor and for the first time incorporate the mandatory provisions relating to the corporate social responsibility. The 2013 Act has introduced several provisions which would change the way the Indian Corporates do business and one such provisions is spending on Corporate Social Responsibility(CSR) activities. Under the New Act a certain percentage of the revenue needs to be mandatorily spent on the welfare of the society, coordinated through a CSR committee. Even though mandatory spending on CSR has been criticised by some corporate houses, but the initiative has been largely welcomed. The concept of Corporate Social Responsibility is governed by Section 135 of the Companies Act, 2013.

However, this Act provide the turning of the Corporate Social Responsibility from voluntary activities to the mandated responsibilities, governed by the bundle of regulations which is as follows:

Section 135 of 2013 Act state that:[24]

1. Every company private limited or public limited, which either has a net worth of rupees five hundred crore or more, or a turnover of rupees one thousand crore or more, or a net profit of rupees five crore or more during any financial year shall constitute a Corporate Social Responsibility Committee of the Board consisting of three or more directors, out of which at least one director shall be an independent director. The CSR activities should not be undertaken in the normal course of business and must be with respect to any of the activities mentioned in Schedule VII of the 2013 Act. Contribution to any political party is not considered to be a CSR activity and only activities in India would be considered for computing CSR expenditure.

Therefore, activities undertaken by the companies as per Schedule VII are as follows:

Activities which may be included by companies in their Corporate Social Responsibility Policies

Activities relating to:—

(i) eradicating extreme hunger and poverty;

(ii) promotion of education;

(iii) promoting gender equality and empowering women;

(iv) reducing child mortality and improving maternal health;

(v) combating human immunodeficiency virus, acquired immune deficiency syndrome, malaria and other diseases;

(vi) ensuring environmental sustainability;

(vii) employment enhancing vocational skills;

(viii) social business projects;

(ix) contribution to the Prime Minister's National Relief Fund or any other fund set up by the Central Government or the State Governments for socioeconomic development and relief and funds for the welfare of the Scheduled Castes, the Scheduled Tribes, other backward classes, minorities and women; and

(x) such other matters as may be prescribed

Further it is provided that the net worth, turnover and net profits are to be computed in terms of Section 198 of the 2013 Act as per the profit and loss statement prepared by the company in terms of Section 381 (1) (a) and Section 198 of the 2013 Act).

1. The Board's report under sub-section (3) of section 134 (o)[25] shall disclose the composition of the Corporate Social Responsibility Committee.

2. The Corporate Social Responsibility Committee shall,

a. formulate and recommend to the Board, a Corporate Social Responsibility Policy which shall indicate the activities to be undertaken by the company as specified in Schedule VII;

b. recommend the amount of expenditure to be incurred on the activities referred to in clause (a); and

c. monitor the Corporate Social Responsibility Policy of the company from time to time.

4. The Board of every company referred to in sub-section (1) shall,

After taking into account the recommendations made by the Corporate Social Responsibility Committee, approve the Corporate Social Responsibility Policy for the company and disclose the contents of such Policy in its report and also place it on the company's website, if any, in such manner as may be prescribed; and ensure that the activities as are included in Corporate Social Responsibility Policy of the company are undertaken by the company.

5. The Board of every company referred to in sub-section (1), shall make every endeavour to ensure that the company spends, in every financial year, at least two per cent of the average net profits of the company made during the three immediately preceding financial years, in pursuance of its Corporate Social Responsibility Policy;

Provided that if the company fails to spend such amount, the Board shall, in its report made under clause (o) of sub-section (3) of section 134[26], specify the reasons for not spending the amount.

Further, Sub Section (8) of Section 134 provides that;

If a company contravenes the provisions of this section, the company shall be punishable with fine which shall not be less than fifty thousand rupees but which may extend to twenty-five lakh rupees and every officer of the company who is in default shall be punishable with imprisonment for a term which may extend to three years or with fine which shall not be less than fifty thousand rupees but which may extend to five lakh rupees, or with both.

4.2.2. Companies (Corporate Social Responsibility Policy) Rules, 2014:[27]

In exercise of the powers conferred under **section 135** and section 469 [sub-sections (1) and (2)] of the Companies Act, 2013 ("Act"), the Central Government, on February 27th (2014), has notified Companies (Corporate Social Responsibility Policy) Rules, 2014 ("CSR Rules"). The Rules, which provides for the implementation for Corporate Social Responsibility ("CSR") obligations, will come into force on 1st April, 2014.

One of the most important features of the CSR Rules is that it defines the term 'Corporate Social Responsibility'; according to Rule 2(c), CSR *means* and *includes but is not limited*

i. Projects or programs relating to activities specified in Schedule VII to the Act; or
ii. (ii) Projects or programs relating to activities undertaken by the board of directors of a company (Board) in pursuance of recommendations of the CSR Committee of the Board as per declared CSR Policy of the company subject to the condition that such policy will cover subjects enumerated in Schedule VII of the Act.

The Draft Rules provide that tax treatment of CSR spend will be in accordance with the Income Tax Act as may be notified by the Central Board of Direct Tax (CBDT).

A separate and exhaustive explanation has also been provided for the concept of "Corporate Social Responsibility" under Rule 3 of CSR Rules which now provides that every company including its holding or subsidiary, and a foreign company defined under section

2(42) of the Act, having its branch office or project office in India, which fulfills the criteria in Section 135(1), shall comply with section 135 of the Act of 2013. This shall be subject to the proviso that net worth, turnover or net profit of a foreign company of the Act shall be computed in accordance with balance sheet and profit and loss account of such company prepared in accordance with Section 381(1)(a) and section 198 of the Act of 2013.

Further, the Rules clarify on a substantial question in themind of many regarding the requirement of a company to comply with the provisions of section 135. **The Rules now clarify that every company which ceases to be a company covered under section 135(1) for three consecutive financial years shall not be required to constitute a CSR committee and to comply with the provisions of Section 135(2) to (5), till such time that it meets the criteria of the thresholds prescribed under section 135(1).**[28]

As per Rule 4 of the CSR Rules, a company shall undertake CSR activities as *projects* or *programs* or *activities.* However, these should not include those activities which a company undertakes *in pursuance of its normal course of business.* Following are other important points concerning CSR activities:

(i) CSR activities can be undertaken through any of the following entities:

(a) A registered trust; or

(b) A registered society; or

(c) A company established by *the company*; or

(d) Its holding or subsidiary or associate company under section 8 of the Act operating within India to facilitate implementation of its CSR activities in accordance with its stated CSR Policy, the following shall apply:

a. The contributing company would need to specify the projects/programs to be undertaken by such an organization, for utilizing funds provided by it;

b. The contributing company shall establish a monitoring mechanism to ensure that the allocation is spent for the intended purpose only;

Collaborations with others Companies:

A Company may also conduct/implement its Corporate Social Responsibility programs through Trusts, Societies, Or Section 8 Companies operating in India, which is not set up by the company itself.

Such spends may be included as part of its prescribed CSR spend only if such organizations have an established track record of at least three years in carrying on activities in related areas.

Companies may collaborate or pool resources with other companies to undertake CSR activities and any expenditure incurred on such collaborative efforts would qualify for computing the CSR spending.

Though Corporate Social Responsibility activities can be undertaken through any of the above entities, there are certain limitations. A company cannot discharge CSR obligations through an entity which is not established by it and does not have an *established track record* of 'three years' in undertaking 'similar programs or projects'.

ii) For undertaking CSR activities, a company can collaborate with other company provided CSR Committees of each of the collaborating companies can *report CSR Activities separately.*

iii) Only CSR activities undertaken in India would amount to 'CSR Expenditure'.

iv) Activities, which only benefit the employees of the companies and their families, would not be considered as the stipulated CSR Activities.

(v) In a single financial year, a company should not spend *more than five percent* of CSR Expenditure in building CSR capacities of its own personnel and implementing agencies.

(vi) Contribution to any *political party* would not be considered as CSR Activity.

CSR Committees

Rule 5 of the CSR Rules obliges the CSR Committee to institute a transparent mechanism to monitor CSR Activities. As provided in the rules, the constitution and composition of the CSR Committee(s) can be explained as follows:

(i) An unlisted public company or a private company, which is not required to appoint an *independent director*, shall have its CSR Committee without such director. Further, a private company, having only two directors, shall constitute its CSR Committee with those two directors.

(ii) So far as foreign company is concerned, the CSR Committee shall comprise of at least two persons with, (i) one person (resident in India) who is authorized to accept on behalf of the company service of process and any notices etc. [Section 380(1)(d) of the Act], and (ii) one person nominated by the concerned foreign company.

CSR Policy

According to Rule 6 of the CSR Rules, CSR Policy of company should include, (i) a list of CSR projects or programs to be undertaken, and (ii) monitoring process of such projects or programs. In addition, it should be specified in the CSR Policy that surplus, arising out of CSR activities, should not form part of the business profit of a company.

CSR Expenditure:

According to Rule 7 of the CSR Rules, CSR Expenditure would include all the expenditure incurred towards CSR activities. However, it would not include the expenditure which is incurred towards an activity not covered under Schedule VII of the Act.

<u>CSR Reporting</u>:

As per Rule 8 of the CSR Rules, the Board's report pertaining to financial year would also include an annual report on CSR obligations. In case of a foreign company, such information should be included as a part of the balance sheet filed under Section 381(1) (b) of the Act but the company shall also contain an Annexure regarding report n CSR by the company.

According to Rule 9 of the CSR Rules, the Board of Directors should disclose the contents of CSR Policy in the report and should also display the same on company's website.

The provisions regarding the display of CSR activities on the company's website remain the same as was provided under the Draft CSR Rules and provide that the Board Of Director shall, after taking into account the recommendations of the CSR Committee, approve the CSR Policy of the company and disclose the contents of such Policy in its report and on the website, if any, as per the particulars described in the Annexure.

The contents of the Annexure provided in the CSR Rules for the reporting of the CSR activities of the company remains the same as was provided under the Draft CSR Rules except that the requirement of mentioning the amount carried forward for the year has been done away with.

Format of Reporting

Format for the annual report on CSR Initiatives to be included in the board report by qualifying companies

¨ Provide a brief outline of the CSR Policy including the statement of intent reflecting the ethos of the company, broad areas of CSR interest and an overview of activities proposed to be undertaken.

¨ Indicate the web-link to the CSR Policy. The Policy should include the full list of projects/activities/programs proposed to be undertaken by the company.

¨ The composition of the CSR Committee.

Contents of CSR Policy

Projects and programmes that are to be undertaken

List of CSR projects/programmes which a company plans to undertake during the implementation year, specifying modalities of execution in the areas/sectors chosen and implementation schedules for the same.

A statement that surplus arising out of the CSR activity will not be part of business profits of a company.

A statement that the corpus would include the following:

a. 2% of the average net profits,
b. any income arising therefrom
c. surplus arising out of CSR activities.

4.2.3. Public Sector Undertakings and Corporate Social Responsibility:

The government of India formed public sector undertakings (PSUs) with the resolution of building industrial capacity, creating employment opportunities and improving the socio-economic condition.

Both, central public sector enterprises (CPSEs) and state level PSUs have played a vital role in supporting the socio-economic development of the country. They are actively involved in various areas of CSR such as education, healthcare, improving infrastructure, social empowerment, vocational training and environmental protection among others.

With a high degree of support from the government, CSPEs acts as a catalyst of social enterprise by providing such diverse services for grass root development.

Over the past two decades, India has emerged as one of the world's strongest emerging markets and PSUs have played a vital role in achieving this growth and development.

In order to sustain this growth, CSR initiatives have become important as they form a crucial part of the companies' strategic decision-making process. In order to integrate this into their business models and achieve the nation's aim of inclusive growth, the Committee of Public Undertaking (COPU) in 1992 examined the issue relating to the social obligations of Central Public Sector Enterprises and observed that "being part of the 'State', every Public Sector Enterprise (PSE) has a moral responsibility to play an active role in discharging the social obligations endowed on a welfare state, subject to the financial health of the enterprise". Based on the recommendation of the COPU, Department of Public Enterprises (DPE) issued general guidelines in November 1994. These guidelines basically left it to the Board of Directors of the PSEs to devise socially responsible business practices in accordance with their Articles of Association, under the general guidance of their respective Administrative Ministry/Department.

In 2009, government made it mandatory for all public sector oil companies to spend 2 per cent of their net profits on corporate social responsibility. To ensure the active participation of public sector companies in CSR initiatives, the government is planning to introduce certain legislations.

The Salient Features of Guideline for Corporate Social Responsibility for Central Public Sector Enterprises (CPSEs) by Ministry of Public Enterprises and Ministry of Heavy Industries which was issued on 9th April 2010 are as follows[29]

1. Planning of CSR Action Plan:

The planning for Corporate Social Responsibility should start with the identification of the activities/projects to be undertaken. Company specific Corporate Social Responsibility strategies should be developed that mandate the design of Corporate Social Responsibility Action Plan (Long-term, medium term and short-term), with a shift from the casual approach to the project based accountability approach. Each of these plans should clearly specify requirements relating to baseline survey; activities to be undertaken, budgets allocated, time-lines prescribed, responsibilities and authorities defined and major results expected.

2. Implementation of CSR Action Plan: CSR initiatives of Central Public Sector Enterprises (CPSEs) should consider the following parameters for identification/ selection of schemes/projects:

• The time-frame and periodic milestones should be finalized at the outset;

• CSR activities should help in building a positive image of the company in the public perception;

• CSR projects may be closely linked with the principles of sustainable development, ensure gender sensitivity, skill enhancement, entrepreneurship development and employment generation by co-creating value with local institutions/people;

• Public-Private Partnership between the Government and the Central Public Sector Enterprise could also be encouraged to leverage the strengths of the latter in Disaster management;

• CSR is to be implemented by Specialized Agencies and generally NOT by staff of the CPSE concerned and

• Activities related to Sustainable Development will form a significant element of the total initiatives of CSR.

3. National CSR Hub: The Department Of Public Enterprises, in conjunction with Standing

Conference of Public Enterprises (SCOPE) and the CPSEs will create a National CSR Hub, which will undertake/facilitate the activities like Nation-wide compilation, documentation, and creation of database; Advocacy; Research; Conferences, Seminars, Workshops - both national and international etc.

4. Monitoring

• Monitoring of the CSR projects is very crucial and needs to be a periodic activity of the Enterprise.
• The Boards of CPSEs should discuss the implementation of CSR activities in their Board meetings.

- CSR projects should also be evaluated by an independent external agency.

Further, the revised CSR and sustainability guidelines were issued by the Department of Public Enterprises (DPE) in December 2012 (effective April 2013) are expected to play a crucial role. The revised guidelines have urged the Central Public Sector Enterprises to clinch a healthy and robust Corporate Social Responsibility practice which is in the interest of all stakeholders. Therefore, the revised guidelines of the Department of Public Enterprises (DPE) inserted the following norms:

CPSEs expected to formulate their policies with a balanced emphasis on all aspects of CSR and Sustainability – equally with regard to their internal operations, activities and processes, as well as in their response to externalities. Earlier guidelines focused mainly on CSR activities for external stakeholders.

Earlier, CSR and sustainable development treated as two separate subject areas and were dealt with differently for the purpose of memorandum of understanding (MoU) evaluation. However, now they are combined into a single set of guidelines for greater transparency.

The revised guideline provides that each CPSE shall with the approval of its Board of Directors make a budgetary allocation for CSR and Sustainability activities/ projects for the year.

The budgetary allocation is determined by the Profit after Tax (PAT) of the company in the previous year:[30]

PAT of CPSE in previous year

Range of Budgetary allocation for CSR and Sustainability activities (as % of PAT in previous year)

i. Less than Rs. 100 crore 3% - 5%

ii. Rs. 100 crore to Rs. 50 2% - 3%
iii. Rs. 500 crore and above 1% - 2%

Thus, for all CPSEs having PAT above Rs. 500 Crores in the previous year, the range of budgetary allocation for CSR and Sustainability activities has been raised to 1%-2%. All CPSEs shall strive to maximize their spending on CSR and Sustainability activities and move towards the higher end of their slabs of budgetary allocation.

The guidelines make it mandatory for all CPSEs to have a two-tier structure, comprising a board level committee headed by either the chairman and managing director, or an independent director, and a group of officers headed by a senior executive not less than one rank below the board level, said the release. This two-tier structure is expected to have the authority and influence to be able to move forward the CSR agenda of the company. The implementation of CSR guidelines is also monitored by the administrative ministry under which the concerned CPSE comes. An appropriate mechanism is being developed for reporting.

CPSEs to take up at least one major project mandatorily for development of a backward district.

CPSEs expected to act in a socially responsible manner at all times. Even in their normal business activities, CPSEs should try to conduct business in a manner that is beneficial to both, business and society.

CPSEs have to disclose the reasons for not fully utilizing the budget allocated for CSR and Sustainability activities for a year. Further, if the CPSEs are unable to spend the earmarked amount for Corporate Social Responsibility in a particular year, it would have to spend the amount in the next two financial years, failing which, it would be transferred to 'Sustainability Fund'.

Emphasis is placed on the scalability of CSR and Sustainability projects, in terms of their size and impact, rather than on their numbers.

Employees to avail the infrastructure facilities created by the company from its CSR and Sustainability budget provided the facilities are originally created essentially for the external stakeholders, and the use of these facilities by the CPSE's employees (internal stakeholders) is only incidental and confined to less than 25 percent of the total number of beneficiaries.

Central Public Sector Enterprises should formulate policies which meet the expectations of the stakeholders, within their organizational resource capability.

In brief, it is generally expected that socially responsible public sector enterprises would take initiatives to:

i. promote organizational integrity and ethical business practices through transparency in disclosure and reporting procedures,

ii. leverage green technologies, processes and standards to produce goods and services that contribute to social and environment sustainability,

iii. contribute to inclusive growth and equitable development in society through capacity building measures, empowerment of the marginalized and underprivileged sections/communities.

iv. promote welfare of employees and labour(casual or contractual), by addressing their concerns of safety, security, professional enrichment and healthy working conditions, whether mandated or otherwise. However, expenditure on mandated activities cannot qualify for CSR's financial components.

v. Central Public Sector Enterprises should formulate policies which meet the expectations of the stakeholders, within their organizational resource capability.

The new guideline has also focused on implementing a robust mechanism for project monitoring. In order to avoid conflict of interest, the guideline enables companies to have a third-party monitoring mechanism. For instance, if a company is implementing CSR projects with the help of its own employees, then for monitoring its implementation it would have to go through a third party and vice-versa. The chart below highlights the key changes in CSR and sustainability guidelines for CPSEs:-[31]

CPSEs reveal improvement in acquiring excellent rating

The aforesaid revised guidelines are in consonance with the National Voluntary Guidelines for Social, Environmental & Economic Responsibilities of Business issued by the Ministry of Corporate Affairs in July 2011 and will stand modified by the provisions of the new Companies Act and updated SEBI Guidelines as and when these are in place and made enforceable.

4. **SEBI - Making Corporate Social Responsibility Reporting Compulsory (Business responsibility reporting)**

SEBI on August13, 2012 has made a mandatory provisions for **top 100 listed companies (by market capitalization)** to report certain critical information as part of their business responsibility.

This includes how much the company is spending on CSR as a percentage of its net profit, the number of stakeholders' complaints received and resolved, details of any pending case filed by stakeholder against any unfair trade practice, irresponsible advertising or anti-competitive behaviour adopted by the company.

The provisions of this circular shall be applicable with effect from financial year ending on or after December 31, 2012.

This will enable the shareholders to have a better understanding of the manner in which their companies' function and adopt responsible business practices.

The circular exhorts the companies to follow the **National Voluntary Guidelines on Social, Environmental and Economic Responsibility[32]** that have been formulated by Ministry of Corporate Affairs in July 2011.

Other listed companies have also been encouraged by SEBI to voluntarily disclose information on their ESG performance in the BRR format.

3. Notable CSR and Sustainability Initiatives[33]

- **Tata Consultancy Services**

The Adult Literacy Program (ALP) was conceived and set up by Dr. F C Kohli along with Prof. P N Murthy & Prof. Kesav Nori of TCS in May 2000 to address the problem of illiteracy. ALP believes illiteracy is a major social concern affecting a third of the Indian population comprising old and young adults. To accelerate the rate of learning, it uses a TCS-designed Computer–Based Functional Literacy Method (CBFL), an innovative teaching strategy that uses multimedia software to teach adults to read within about 40 learning hours.

- **Larsen & Toubro (L & T) Limited**

Considering that construction industry is the second largest employer in India after agriculture, employing about 32 million-strong workforce, L&T set out to regulate and promote Construction Vocational Training (CVT) in India by establishing a Construction Skills Training Institute (CSTI) on a 5.5 acre land, close to its Construction Division Headquarters at Manapakkam, Chennai. CSTI imparts, totally free of cost, basic training in formwork, carpentry, masonry, bar-bending, plumbing and sanitary, scaffolder & electrical wireman trades to wide spectrum of the rural poor.

CSTI has also set up a branch at Panvel, Mumbai, initially offering training in formwork, carpentry and masonry trades. The Manapakkam and Panvel facilities together provide training to about 300 candidates annually who are inducted after a process of selection, the minimum qualification being tenth standard. Since inception, these two units have produced about 2,000 skilled workmen in various trades, with about sixty percent of them being deployed to L&T's jobsites spread across the country.

- **ITC Limited**

ITC partnered the Indian farmer for close to a century. ITC is now engaged in elevating this partnership to a new paradigm by leveraging information technology through its trailblazing 'e-Choupal' initiative. ITC is significantly widening its farmer partnerships to embrace a host of value-adding activities:

- Creating livelihoods by helping poor tribals make their wastelands productive;
- Investing in rainwater harvesting to bring much-needed irrigation to parched dry lands;
- Empowering rural women by helping them evolve into entrepreneurs; and
- Providing infrastructural support to make schools exciting for village children.

Through these rural partnerships, ITC touches the lives of nearly 3 million villagers across India.

- **CISCO System Inc.**

The company pursues a strong "triple bottom line" which is described as profits, people and presence. It promotes a culture of charitable giving and connects employees to nonprofit organizations serving the communities where they live. It invests its best-in-class networking equipment to those nonprofit organizations that best put it to work for their communities, eventuating in positive global impact. It takes its responsibility seriously as a global citizen. Education is a top corporate priority for Cisco, as it is the key to prosperity and opportunity. Thus,

Successfuls corporations distribute resources to ensure well-being of stakeholders which also enables the company to acquire a key differentiator vis-à-vis its competition, thereby making the business sustainable.

- Tata Chemicals and HUL pioneered iodization of salt to combat iodine deficiency. Their market campaign to change the mindset of BPL customers to pay a little extra for the pack of iodized salt was clearly laudable.

These efforts not only increased their market share and profitability but at the same time addressed an important nutritional issue of national importance.

- Hindustan Unilever (HUL), for example, invests in research working with nutrition and health specialists to further improve its "ready to eat" food business, enhance hygiene through its "regular hand wash" campaign, etc. These initiatives not only position its products distinctively against the competitors and enhance brand equity, but also ensure well-being of customers and the environment.
- ITC

In order to combat the global shortage of pulp-wood for paper board production, ITC and Ballarpur Industries are helping small farmers with degraded land pieces by providing them saplings, financial and technical support and an assured buy back of timber. This ensures sustainable raw material supply for the company, and also improves farmer's livelihood.

Thus, social initiatives can also help in enhancing ethical values in society and at the same time can offer a distinctive perimeter to corporations.

- Fluor Corporation, one of the largest construction companies in the world, worked for three decades with Transparency International to fight corruption; today its "anti-corruption" movement has 150 large companies across industries having signed a "zero-tolerance" policy on bribery. In industries marred by corruption, Flour is today perceived as an ethical player, thereby positioning itself with a significant competitive advantage.

- Maruti has recently adopted forty Industrial Training Institutes (ITI) which not only enhances skill level of youth making them employable, but also guarantees supply of skilled personnel to Maruti. Similar investments in skills development training are made by companies like Microsoft, Infosys, Tata Steel and L&T.

Thus, rather than paying donations, using core strengths to address social issues is the best form of sustainable corporate social responsibility.

4. Criticism of Sections 135 of the Companies Act 2013:

A bare reading of the new CSR rules may indicate simplicity and reader-friendliness. But close analysis of the rules leaves abundant room for vagueness at various places.

While the Companies Act prescribes a specific method for computing net profits and the CSR contribution, the CSR rules take a step backwards in figure out exclusions from the net profit so calculated. Most outrageously, one of the exclusions provides that the profits of a branch of an Indian company located outside India cannot be merged into the profits of the parent company for the purpose of computing the 2% contribution. This exclusion goes against the very mandate of Section 135 and as such, ultra vires to that extent.

Secondly, there appears to be a major contradiction in the rules in respect of the meaning of the words 'corporate social responsibility'. The Companies Act, 2013, defines CSR activities to mean an identified set of activities demarcated in the separate schedule to the Act. However, a reading of the definition indicates that the list of CSR activities provided in the rules (which also includes the schedule activities) is only illustrative and not exhaustive. At the same time, an overall reading of the rules strongly suggests that the scheduled activities alone will be considered for the purpose of Corporate Social Responsibility.

Another aspect of ambiguity in the new law that was expected to be corrected through the rules was the 'local area preference'. The Act provides that a company should give preference to the local area in which it operates for CSR spending. How would this work if a company has more than one operational office in the same city, or even otherwise? Is the location of a factory, as opposed to the corporate office, the target of preference?

The CSR rules have rightly excluded contributions directly or indirectly made to a political party from the scope of CSR activity. But, what about contributions made to institutions affiliated with one or more politicians or those located in a constituency represented by a politician who has some form of regulatory supervision or leverage over that company? What about activities/institutions being run under the trusteeship or office of a politician?

Another aspect of the rules that may be abused is the carve-out made in respect of CSR activities undertaken 'only' for the benefit of the employees and their families. Could the intent of the legislation have been to mean activities undertaken 'primarily' to benefit the employees? If a company undertakes a project primarily but not exclusively benefiting its employees, should that be considered CSR activity? While the new rules are well-meaning, there is definitely room for further clarity and certainty. The last thing anyone wants is a select group of people with vested interests benefiting from this noble legislative initiative.

The Act does not prescribe any penal provision if a company fails to spend amount on CSR activities. The Board will need to explain reasons for non-compliance in its report.

Further, Section 149 of the Act mandates only public companies whether listed or in other prescribed class to have Independent Directors.

In contrast, applicability of CSR requirements depends on net worth, turn over or net profit criterion, irrespective of whether the company is a public or private company.

Every company covered by CSR needs to constitute a CSR committee with at least one independent director.

This implies that even a private company will need to have an independent director if it is covered under CSR requirements.

Even central public sector enterprises, subject to CSR norms under separate guidelines, will, on enactment of the bill, come within the purview of these new provisions.

Another, ambiguity on the Act is the Tax treatment to CSR spending by companies whether it is to be treated as non-deductible income since it is an allocation of profit, or, whether it is to be treated as an allowable expenditure under the Income Tax Act.

Section 80G of Income Tax Act – Donations

This section does not restrict the deduction to individuals, companies or any specific category of taxpayer and is allowable to all kind of assessee.

Donations made to foreign trusts do not quality for deduction under this section.

Deduction cannot be claimed for donations made to political parties for any reason, including paying for brochures, souvenirs or pamphlets brought out by such parties.

Only donation made to prescribed funds and institutions qualify for deduction.

Maximum allowable deduction:- If aggregate of the sums donated exceed 10% of the adjusted gross total income, the amount in excess of 10% ceases to be entitled for tax benefit.

Only donations in cash/ cheque are eligible for the tax deduction.

NRIs are also entitled to claim tax benefits against donations, subject to the donations being made to eligible institutions and funds.

Further, Section 35 AC of Income Tax Act – Expenditure on eligible projects/ schemes

To promote reinvestment of business profits in areas where massive capital input is required for socio-economic development, a tax incentive has been provided under Section 35AC of the Income Tax Act, 1961.

The section provides that where an assessee incurs any expenditure by way of payments of any sum to:

i) a public sector company or;

ii) a local authority or;

iii) to an association/ institution approved by the National Committee for carrying out any eligible project or scheme for promoting the social and economic welfare or upliftment of the public as the Central Government may specify, then the amount so paid shall be allowed as deduction from the business income of the assessee/ contributor of such amount.

In the absence of specific provision for deductibility of CSR expenditure, whether the deduction can be allowed under Section 37of the Income-tax Act, 1961?

Does it make any difference to the proposition if expenditure is perceived to be a capital expenditure?

If considered to be deductible, in which year would the expense be deductible? Can deduction be claimed on the basis of provision towards CSR, without having actually incurred?

Lastly, it is also criticized on the basis that the Act ignores the Corporate Affairs Ministry's very comprehensive national voluntary guidelines (NVGs) on social, environmental and economic responsibilities of business.

5. CONCLUSION:

Thus, CSR is becoming a fast-developing and increasingly competitive field. "Putting CSR into operation, bringing it to the heart of corporate culture without losing sight of core business objectives, while also avoiding the traps of paternalism and philanthropy, is like getting into a new world of humanity and brotherhood. It is step forward with the idealism and philosophy as enshrined in the "Preamble of our Constitution". Corporate Social Responsibility is not only relevant because of a changing policy environment but also because of its ability to meet business objectives. Notification of Section 135, Companies (Corporate Social Responsibility Policy) Rules 2014 has come at a time when the corporate world was in much conjecture of the far reaching effects of the new Act, its provisions and the resulting increase in responsibilities and role. A pro- community initiative and a mandatory responsibility of the companies reaching

[1]*Michael Porter and Mark Kramer, Harvard Business Review, Dec., 2006*

[2] *I.Const. Article 38,*

[3] *I. Const. Article 39(1)(a)*

[4] *I.Const.Article 39(1)(b)*

[5] *I.Const. Article 39 (1)(c)*

[6] *I.Const. Article 41*

[7] Inserted by the Constitution (Forty-second Amendment) Act, 1976, s. 11 (w.e.f. 3-1-1977)

[8]*Id.* at Article 51A (g),

[9]*Id.* at Article 51A (h),

[10]*Id.* at Article 51A (j),

[11] AIR 1963 SC 1811

[12] See also *Dwarkadas Shrinivas of Bombay* v. *The Sholapur Spinning & Waving Co. Ltd.*, [1954] 1 SCR 674; *The Bengal Immunity Company Limited* v. *The State of Bihar*, [1955] 2 SCR 603; *Chiranjit Lal Chowdhuri* v. *The Union of India* [1950] 1 SCR 869; *Louis De Readt* v. *Union of India*, (1991) 3 SCC 554; *Deena alias Deen Dayala and Ors.* v. *Union of India and Ors.* AIR 1983 SC 1155; *Indo China Steam Navigation Co. Ltd.* v. *Jasjit Singh*, AIR 1964 SC 1140

[13] 1983 (1) SCR 922. In *Workmen of Meenakshi Mills Ltd* v. *Meenakshi Mills Ltd.*, 1992 (3) SCC, 336, the right of the management to declare lay off under s.25-N of the Industrial Disputes Act, 1984 under Article 19(1)(g) of the Constitution are subject to the mandates containing Arts.38, 39A, 41 and 43. Therefore, right under Article 19(1)(g) was held to be subject to the directive principles. Similarly,

[14] JT 1995 (1) SC 637

[15] AIR 1995 SC 1811

[16] 1989(2) SCR 751

[17] (1991)1 SCC 212, para 22

[18] (1993)1 SCC 445 at page 464 para 28

[19] W.P.No.802 of 2009

[20] Press Information Bureau, Ministry of Petroleum and Natural Gas, Government of India, Oil PSUs agree to spend two per cent of profits on Social Responsibilities, Feb. 2, 2009 available at http://pib.nic.in/newsite/erelease.aspx?relid=47172.

[21] Ministry of Corporate Affairs, Corporate Social Responsibility Voluntary Guidelines, 2009, available at http://www.mca.gov.in/Ministry/latestnews/CSR_Voluntary_Guidelines_24dec2009.pdf.

[22] Press Information Bureau, Ministry of Corporate Affairs, Government of India, Corporate Social Responsibility, 11 Aug. 2011 available at http://pib.nic.in/newsite/erelease.aspx?relid=74428.

[23] *www.mca.gov.in/Ministry/**companies_act**.html*

[24]*http://www.business-standard.com*

[25] Under Clause (o) of Sub-Section (3) of Section 134;There shall be attached to statements laid before a company in a general meeting, a report by its Board of Directors, which shall include:

(o) The details about the policy developed and implemented by the company on corporate social responsibility initiatives taken during the year

[26] Ibid.

[27] www.mca.gov.in/Ministry/**pdf/companiesactnotifications2-2014.pdf**

[28] http://www.companiesact.in/PGInformation/NewsDetailsInfor.aspx?385#sthash.YfsjNPvK.dpuf

[29] Prabhash Dalei and Pravesh Dalei, Corporate Social Responsibility in India, International Conference on Humanities, Geography and Economics (ICHGE'2011) Pattaya Dec. 2011 also available at http://dpe.nic.in/newgl/glch1223.pdf

[30] The revised guideline by DPE, with effect from April2013,www.dpemou.nic.in/

MOUFiles/**Revised_CSR_Guidelines**.pdf

[31] Guidelines on Corporate Social Responsibility and *Sustainability for Central Public Sector Enterprises*

http://www.recindia.nic.in/download/DPE_Guide-lines_CSR_Sust.pdf

[32] The nine principles of National Voluntary Guidelines are:

Principle 1: Businesses should conduct and govern themselves with ethics, transparency and accountability.

Principle 2: Businesses should provide goods and services that are safe and contribute to sustainability throughout their life cycle.

Principle 3: Businesses should promote the wellbeing of all employees.

Principle 4: Businesses should respect the interests of, and be responsive toward all stakeholders, especially those who are disadvantaged, vulnerable and marginalized.

Principle 5: Businesses should respect and promote human rights.

Principle 6: Business should respect, protect, and make efforts to restore the environment.

Principle 7: Businesses, when engaged in influencing public and regulatory policy, should do so in a responsible manner.

Principle 8: Businesses should support inclusive growth and equitable development.

Principle 9: Businesses should engage with and provide value to their customers and consumers in a responsible manner.

[33] S. Ravi, FCA, 'Overview of Corporate Social Responsibility'

CHAPTER FIVE

INDIAN JUDICIARY on Corporate Social Responsibility

5.1. Introduction:

With the shifting of the corporate social responsibility paradigm to a stakeholder centric approach, practices at the ground level have also undergone a radical transformation. In every aspect of corporate social responsibility measures the last decade has seen corporations innovating to increase efficiency, effectiveness and accountability. The change is evident in the statements about corporate social responsibility being made by India's leading industrial groups like the Tata's, *"over the years, the nature of the company's involvement with the community has undergone a change. It has moved away from charity and dependence to empowerment and partnership"* [1]and the consistent transformation in their corporate social responsibility practices in the last decade. The focus has been on initiatives that are people-centric with active community participation at all levels, like giving financial grants or sponsorships to providing products and services in a manner that would make a real difference in the target communities. However, the real revolution occurred at the implementation stages where companies have started committing manpower, expertise in addition to financial resources in order to provide a host of services, programs and schemes that are flexible enough to accommodate the needs of the target community and also see greater people participation at all stages and tighter accountability standards. It has also been emphasized by the Indian Prime Minister, Manmohan Singh that:

"Corporate social responsibility must not be defined by tax planning strategies alone. Rather, it should be defined within the framework of a corporate philosophy which factors the needs of the community and the regions in which a corporate entity functions. This is part of our cultural Heritage. Mahatma Gandhi called it trusteeship....I invite corporate India to be a Partner in making ours a more humane and just society... We need a new Partnership for Inclusive Growth based on what I describe as a Ten Point Social Charter...first, we need to have healthy respect for your workers and invest in their welfare..."

The first perceptible change has been the introduction of a host of innovative programs and schemes in several areas like education, healthcare, rural development, environment protection, protection of artistic and cultural heritage and disaster management that are customized to meet the specific needs of the target group and corporations devote not only financial resources but expertise, manpower, products and services for the successful implementation of these schemes:

• Lupin India Ltd, India's third largest manufacturer of pharmaceuticals has started a project for providing sustainable development in 154 villages across Rajasthan.

The scheme instead of providing for piece-meal assistance that does not lead to effective alleviation of poverty or adequate development is designed as a holistic action plan that includes an Agricultural Income

Generation Scheme, land cultivation and fruit plantation programs, fodder preservation schemes, sericulture and water-recycling programs, establishment of medical and educational centers, adult literacy programs and credit schemes.

• Cipla, another Indian pharmacy has found a novel approach to fulfill its corporate social responsibility obligations by offering to sell a cocktail of three anti-HIV drugs, Stavudine, Lamivudine and Nevirapine, to the Nobel Prize-winning voluntary agency Medicine Sans Frontieres (MSF) at a rate of $350, and at $600 per patient per year to other NGOs over the world. This offer has to led to an significant decrease in the prices of these drugs worldwide increasing the accessibility of these drugs especially in the developing countries.

• Ranbaxy, one of India's major pharmaceutical firms operates seven mobile healthcare vans and two urban welfare centers that reach over a lakh people in various parts of northern and central India as part of its corporate social responsibility initiative.

• Tata Consultancy Services (TCS) has set up a fully-equipped computer training laboratory for children from the Society for the Welfare of the Physically Handicapped and Research Centre, in Pune for imparting basic computer knowledge. NIIT has launched a highly popular 'hole-in-the-wall' scheme where it places a computer on a public wall in urban and rural areas so that neighborhood children can learn computer basics using the play-way method.

• Bharat Electronics Ltd built cyclone proof houses for the victims of the super cyclone in with the help of the victims themselves so that the houses are built according to their needs.

• Ion Exchange has founded a profitable venture for environmental protection through water treatment, afforestation and organic farming

Thus, a bundle of initiatives have been undertaken by the corporations (either private or public) and governments in the field of Corporate Social Responsibility. However, the actual paradigm shifting from charity and dependence to empowerment and partnership has not been implemented. The corporations mainly focus on the thematic areas only instead of focusing on the empowerment and partnership. They basically restrict their CSR initiatives by giving financial grants or sponsorships in several areas like education, healthcare, rural development, environment protection, protection of artistic and cultural heritage and disaster management. This is somewhat known as an indirect charity and making their stakeholders or employees dependent, instead of empowering them. Empowerment means creating an environment where people are equipped and encouraged to make decisions in autonomous ways and to feel that they are in control of the outcomes for which they are responsible. It means opening the door for dissent, avoiding groupthink and encouraging innovation. Thus, by distributing authority throughout the organization the individuals are said to be empowered in a real sense. Today the companies are merely giving an indirect charity to their employees, stakeholders, etc. in the name of CSR policies. For instance, the government MANREGA policy is the glaring example of an indirect charity for the sake of CSR policy which aims to guarantee the 'right to work' and ensure livelihood security in rural areas by providing at least 100 days of guaranteed wage employment in a financial year to every household whose adult members volunteer to do unskilled manual work. Thus, by providing this 100days of guaranteed wage employment to individuals the governments are indirectly making them dependent and disabled. The policy mainly focuses on charity and dependence inspite of empowering the individuals. Therefore, many corporations as well as government are in the name of CSR initiatives undertake the policies which fundamentally efforts on charity and making stakeholders, employees, as well as customers dependent instead of empowering and making them independent. The significant roles on this line is made by the Satyam **Computer Services** by giving its shares to its employees and stakeholders in the company and make their participation in the companies affairs by arranging group level employees participations. Thus, through this initiative they empowered its stakeholders and employees and develop with them an active partnership policy. Therefore, the shareholders and creditors are empowered and the employees enjoy the improved systems of management and the community at large enjoys the fruits of better economic growth in a responsible way.

5.2. Indian judiciary on Corporate Social Responsibility:

Judiciary has a significant role in controlling the perils of uncontrolled developments, satisfying the needs of the present generations and at the same time ensuring that the resource of future generations is not jeopardized. Indian judiciary also plays a vital role in enhancing the policy of Corporate Social Responsibility.

Union Carbide Corporation vs. Union of India popularly known as Bhopal Gas Disaster Case[2]

The 1984 Bhopal Gas disaster involved a calamitous failure at Union Carbide Corporation (UCC), pesticide manufacturing plant at Bhopal, India. Over 15,000 people died, and 500,000 injured in the accident. The disaster occurred due to lack of safety measures and inferior technology at the plant. The aftermath of the disaster was improperly handled by the management of UCC as well as Dow Chemical after its takeover. Indian government officials also failed to provide ample compensation and relief and rehabilitation to the victims. It had been the source of constant legal battles in both India and the U.S. that Dow being financially sound could have dealt the case on much humanitarian ground but it denied to take any liability and responsibility of the disaster. This disaster raises some serious corporate social responsibility issues to be addressed by manufacturing Companies, in their responsibility towards the community and environment as well, and should examines the economic, and legal aspects and addresses the wider issues facing the stakeholders and the players. This accident brings to us many sociol as well as legal issues that are much diverse than those encountered in other industrial or environmental disasters. This accident is incomparable, not because of the high number of human casualties or the long-term ill effects on the health of the populace of that area, but because this accident raised questions of social responsibility and that were only feared and dealt with marginally in international resolutions and the Code of Conduct for Transnational Corporations.

Therefore, having seen the collision of negligence on the part of both the management as well as government in order to look into the environmental, safety and compensatory aspect, Bhopal Gas Leak Disaster (Processing of Claims) Act, 1985 and Environmental Protection Act of 1986 were enacted. Though the former Act gave all powers to the Central Government to represent all claimants in appropriate forums, appreciable result did not come out even after 20 years.

Thus the proper and structured corporate social responsibility (CSR) approaches to deal with the similar case was indirectly evolved and since then judiciary always through its interpretations check the corporation's uncontrolled, hazardous and ignorant practices towards their stakeholders and society as a whole.

The tremendous pressure on the Indian government after Bhopal Gas Tragedy[3] and Oleum Gas Leak[4]lead to the evolution of jurisprudence of Corporate Social Responsibility in which the judiciary played vital role. However, the issues which were left unanswer in the previous two cases, the Supreme court in the case of Charan Lal Sahu[5] manifest the judgment which was significant and instrumental in the enactment of various acts in this regard. The court in this case first of all held the Bhopal Gas Leak Disaster (Processing of Claims) Act, 1985[6] to be constitutionally valid. The court considered the doctrine of parens patria[7] and on the basis of it justified the act of the government. The most important pronouncement of the court in this case was with regards to rules and regulations for hazardous substances and dealt with environmental legislations, steps to be taken by the govt., responsibilities of citizen and the corporations. The court observed: -

• "Creation of fund for disaster in which contribution from the industry is mandatory and upon the government can grant the licence subject to the condition that all other conditions are fulfilled.

• The basis for damages in case of leakages and accident should be statutorily fixed taking into consideration the nature of damages inflicted, the consequences thereof and the ability and capacity of the parties to pay. Such law should also provide for deterrent or punitive damages, the basis for which should be formulated by an expert committee or by the government: 'This' (the court said) 'is vital for the future.'

• A law should be enacted to ensure immediate relief to victims - viz. by providing for the constitution of tribunals regulated by special procedure for determining compensation to victims of industrial disasters or accident, appeals against which may lie to the Supreme Court on limited questions of law, and only after depositing the amount determined by the tribunal.

• The law should also provide for interim relief to victims during the pendency of proceedings: these steps would minimize the misery and agony of victims of hazardous enterprises.

• The law should provide for the establishment of a statutory 'Industrial Disaster Fund', contributions to which may be made by the government and industries, whether they are of transnational corporations or domestic undertakings, public or private. The fund should be permanent in nature, so that the money is readily available for providing immediate effective relief to the victims. This would avoid delay in providing effective relief to the victims.

The Supreme Court in **M.C. Mehta v. Kamal Nath[8]** elucidated that compensating degradation of environment caused due to non-adherence to the prescribed standards was different than being penalized for causing pollution and non-compliance with statutory obligation. Remedial and restoration measures in relation to degradation of environment resulting from default and the money spent would squarely come under the head of compensation.

In the recent case of **M.C. Mehta v. Union of India (UOI) and Ors**[9] concerning the Environment degradation caused by mining activity in Aravalli Hills. NEERI[10] was sought on point whether mining operations in area to be stopped in interest of environmental protection, pollution control and tourism development. On consideration of reports, Supreme Court holding that mining activities in vicinity of tourist resorts was bound to cast serious impact on local ecology directed for stopping mining operations within 2 kms. Radius of tourist resorts of Badkal Lake and Surajkund and that mining leases not to be renewed without prior no objection certificate from HPCB and also from Central Pollution Control.

In **Consumer Education & Research Centre v. Union of India**[11] 'right' of the management in asbestos industry to carry on its business is subject to their obligation to 'protect health of the workmen', 'preserve pollution free atmosphere', and to 'provide safe and healthy conditions of the workmen'.

In **National Textile Workers' Union vs. P.R. Ramakrishna**[12]the Apex Court held that the traditional view that a company is the property of the shareholders is an exploded myth. According to the new socio-economic thinking, a company is a social institution having duties and responsibilities towards the community in which it functions. Obviously the Hon'ble Supreme Court of India is referring to CSR, when it talks of 'duties and responsibilities' towards the community. The generally accepted view is that if a company has the resources and has come a long way in its progress, it owes a debt to the society and the community in which it has progressed. Also, it is agreed that if a company has caused some loss to its surrounding areas, it is its obligation to make up for that loss, whether technical or environmental, as a part of its CSR

Panchmahals Steel Ltd. vs. Universal Steel Traders[13]

In this case, the Gujarat High Court has pointed out that a company has three-fold reality:

•Economic reality

•Human reality, and

• Public reality, and the company is duty-bound to take-up this initiatives in order to give back to the society.

Birla Zauri Agro Chemical Ltd., Goa Case[14]:

In this case, the Goa High Court ordered the closure of the company's operations because the effluents of the company were polluting the sea causing large-scale deaths of fish and also polluting the wells of villagers and damaging the crops. Here the company was obviously violating the environment laws. The company has a statutory duty in such cases to take care of the pollutants and maintain the environmental balance. It follows the principle that the polluter pays. As a responsible corporate citizen, the company should have set up an effluent treatment plant not only as a part of its statutory obligations but also in fulfillment of its CSR objectives.

On 22 September, 2011 The Madras High Court while dealing with **Bears Cave Estate vs. The Presiding Officer, Labour Court, Salem.[15]** referred the case of **Kunal Singh vs. Union of India[16]**. Wherein, the Supreme Court observed thus: Section 47 contains a clear directive that the employer shall not dispense with or reduce in rank an employee who acquires a disability during the service. In construing a provision of a social beneficial enactment that too dealing with disabled persons intended to give them equal opportunities, protection of rights and full participation. Section 47 is casting statutory obligation on the employer to protect an employee acquiring disability during service. Further it held that, the principles behind suffering a person with disabilities are that providing equal opportunities cannot be left only for the mercy by the Government in relation to its servants alone. It is high time the principles behind the Disabilities Act, 1955 must be extended in relation to private employments also and it must be made as part of Corporate Social responsibility of every employee.

In the case **of M/s. Live Oak Resort P. Ltd. and anr v. Panchgani Hill Station Municipal Council** [17]the appellants had been that there was large scale illegal construction and deforestation in the Mahabaleshwar-Panchgani region resulting in wide spread environmental and ecological degradation to these two hill stations in the State of Maharashtra. The Court said giving importance to the forest reserve and deliberating on the effects of deforestation held that that the two hill stations of Panchgani and Mahabaleshwar recently have been acclaimed to be very popular tourist resorts and tourism has thus turned out to be a great economic benefactor to the State.

In the case of **M/s Aziz timber corp. v. State of Jammu & Kashmir**[18]the petitioners, M/S Aziz Timber Corporation and others, are involved in logging in the State of Jammu and Kashmir. In that State there was a significant problem with deforestation and illegal logging, and thus, pursuant to Writ Petition the Supreme Court of India delivered an order imposing a logging ban within the state. The Supreme Court of India also prohibited the removal from the State of any trees that had been cut, and directed the Chief Secretary of the State of Jammu and Kashmir to ensure strict and faithful compliance with this order.

State Pollution Control Board, Odisha Represented through its Member-Secretary vs. M/s. Swastik Ispat Pvt. Ltd., Represented through its Director, Senior Branch Manager and Indian Overseas Bank and Central Pollution Control Board[19]

In this case, the industry had failed to discharge it corporate social responsibility. It had done damage to the environment which it was liable to make good and decided to invoke the Bank Guarantee rather than issuing directions for closure of the unit. Thus, it was held that invocation of bank guarantee by Board for non-compliance of conditions stated in consent order would not be held to be penal and impermissible under provisions of Air Act - Therefore Board would be entitled to receive guarantee amount, however, would be entitled to use same only for purposes of making good environmental loss or degradation caused by Applicant.

The Tata Power Company Limited (Transmission) Vs.Maharashtra Electricity Regulatory State Commission[20]

In this case it was argued whether disallowance of Operation and Mismanagement (O&M) expenses with respect to Corporate Social Responsibility Expenditure in Financial Years 2009-10 and 2010-11 was justified - Held, Community Social Responsibility was responsibility of Company - In fact, State Commission was duty bound to apply prudency check while truing up otherwise no purpose would be served in truing up. The State Commission is of the view that these costs are towards Tata Power Company's Corporate Social Responsibility and are not necessary for the functioning of any Utility. In any case, these expenses should not be passed on to the consumers of Tata Power Company as the consumers are not benefiting from the same and thus, these expenses should be borne by Tata Power Company.

Antarsingh Patel vs. Union of India[21]

In this case it was held that citizens are at the center of development and as such all efforts are required to be made to avoid any hardships to the affected persons. It is in this context, that the Project Proponent must provide facilities under the Corporate Social Responsibility (CSR) to the affected persons. These facilities, under CSR activity, must include health, education, skill-development, employment-opportunities, improvement in infrastructure facilities etc. Adequate funds for CSR should be earmarked for this purpose by the Project Proponent. Progress made in this regard should be monitored by MoEF and State Government.

In the case of **Udaipur Mineral Development Syndicate (P) Limited[22], the** Hon'ble Rajasthan High Court has held that the moment the assesse digs the pits for mining he is legally bound to fill those pits and the liability accrues on the very date when the pits are due.

As held by the Apex Court in **Vellore Citizens' Welfare Forum vs. Union of India** and others[23], sustainable development needs to be maintained and at the same time the entrepreneurs have to shoulder corporate social responsibility (CSR) which are held to be inseparable twins,

As held in **G. Sundarrajan vs. Union of India**[24]and **M.C. Mehta vs. Union of India**[25]By stoppage of the mining operations, the mining activities will come to a standstill, throwing the operations of the lessees haywire and putting the interests of thousands of workers and employees living on these operations in jeopardy.

Power System Operation Corporation Limited, New Delhivs. Users under the category of Distribution Licensees and Buyers CMD, UPPCL, Uttar Pradesh Power Corporation Limited, Shakti Bhawan, 14-Ashok Marg, Lucknow- 226001 and Ors.[26]

The court held that as per the directives of Department of Public Enterprises, Government of India making it mandatory for all CPSEs to enter into MoU with their administrative ministries and the subsidiary companies with their holding company to carry out mandatory activities under Corporate Social Responsibility (CSR), Sustainable Development (SD) and R&D by meeting the expenditure as a percentage of profit after tax of the CPSE. Accordingly, the petitioner has prayed for allowing the expenditure on these activities by relaxing Regulation 9(3) of RLDC Fees and Charges Regulations. GUVNL has opposed the expenditure on the ground that NLDC and RLDC being load despatch centres and discharging statutory responsibilities under the Act cannot be termed as CPSE and therefore, expenditure on CSR and SD should not be allowed. However, it is held that, it is a mandatory requirement for a subsidiary company to enter into MoU with its Holding company as per the guidelines of DPE. Therefore, POSOCO which is a 100% subsidiary of PGCIL cannot escape the responsibility to sign MoU with PGCIL. In terms of the MoU, it is obligated to undertake CSR, SD and R&D activities.

5.3. <u>CONCLUSION-</u>

Indian Judiciary is playing vital role in reminding the corporate world of its CSR towards the society where from it is being existed. The judiciary always acts as a sword in order to pierce the corporate evil practices. The first major check on corporate practices was made out in the case of M.C. Mehta vs. Union of India popularly known as Olieum Gas Leak case where the Supreme Court propounded the principle of Absolute liability of the corporations. It was debated vehemently before this court with regards to the liability of an enterprise engaged in the hazardous or inherently dangerous substance. The court upheld that Law is not only proactive but also reactive at the same time, the old doctrine was no longer able to cope up with the changing scenario and hence a need was felt for the judicial creativity to plug - in the loopholes. Further the t court observe that, where an enterprise is engaged in a hazardous or inherently dangerous activity and harm results to anyone on account of an accident in the operation of such hazardous or inherently dangerous activity resulting, for example, in escape of toxic gas the enterprise is strictly and absolutely liable to compensate all those who are affected by the accident and such liability is not subject to any of the exceptions which operate vis-à-vis the tortious principle of strict liability[27] under the rule in Rylands v. Fletcher.[28] This was the evolution of the doctrine of absolute liability in our country. In the Bhopal Gas Tragedy case the apex court for the first time put emphasis on the Social Responsibility of the corporations toward society, their shareholders, customers and the State also.

The apex court upheld that the traditional goals of corporation have been profits, sales and wealth maximization. Now, profit is still the main motive of the corporation but it is not the sole motive as the role of contemporary corporations has been to serve the society at large, since it uses societal resources, namely man power and raw material. Justice P. N. Bhagwati has aptly remarked in this connection that maximization of social welfare should be the legitimate goal of a company.

[1] www.tatasteel.com

[2] 1990 AIR 273, 1989 SCC (2) 540.

[3] 1990 AIR 273, 1989 SCC (2) 540.

[4] AIR 1987 SC 1086

[5] 1990 (1) SCC 613.

[6] Order of the Madhya Pradesh High Court, Dated April 4, 1988, at http://www.lloyd-jones.net/Kalpana/Bhopal-3.htm

[7] . Parens patriae is Latin for "father of the people". In law, it refers to the public policy power of the state to usurp the rights of the natural parent, legal guardian or informal carer, and to act as the parent of any child or individual who is in need of protection, such as a child whose parents are unable or unwilling to take care of him or her, or an incapacitated and dependent individual

[8] (MANU/SC/0416/2000: AIR 2000 SC 1997)

[9] AIR2004SC4016, 2004(3)SCALE396, (2004)12SCC118

[10] National Environmental Engineering Research Institute

[11] JT 1995 (1) SC 637

[12] 1983 (1) SCR 922.

[13] 1976 46 CompCas 706 Guj, (1975) GLR 942

[14] **(April 1975)**

[15] **W.P.No.802 of 2009**

[16] 524 (D/13.02.2003).

[17] [2001] RD-SC 448 (31 August 2001)

[18] O.W.P. No. 568-84/96

[19]MANU/GT/0001/2014Appeal No. 68 of 2012

[20]MANU/ET/0150/2013, Appeal No. 104 of 2012

[21]MANU/GT/0071/2012

[22]   MANU/RH/0771/2002   :   [2003]   261   ITR 706(Raj.)

[23] MANU/SC/0686/1996 : (1996) 5 SCC 647

[24] MANU/SC/0466/2013 : (2013) 6 SCC 620

[25] MANU/SC/0768/2009 : (2009) 6 SCC 142.

[26] Petition No. 200/MP/2011 with I.A. No. 16/2012

[27] . Liability without fault; also known as liability without regard to fault or strict liability. Absolute liability is imposed in various states when actions of an individual or business are deemed contrary to public policy, even though an action may not have been intentional or negligent.

[28] See, (1868) [1] LR 3 HL 330

Suggestions/recommendations & Conclusion

SUGGESTIONS/RECOMMENDATIONS & CONCLUSION
SUGGESTIONS & RECOMMENDATIONS

The suggestions/recommendations made by me are as follows[1]:

1. Corporate Social Responsibility should undertake *"Inclusive development"* norm as an agenda:

Section 135 (5) of the Act provides that *"the company shall give preference to the local area and areas around it where it operates for spending the CSR resources"*. Although this is a welcoming step to build a stronger community-business relationship, but it may rotate resource sharing by undermining *"inclusive development"* norm. While most of the corporate communities and their industrialized amenities are located mostly in the comparatively well to do states, resource requirement is more in the under developed states where there are no-industries such as the North-Eastern states and others. A similar situation also arises when we consider intra-state enlargement necessities and location of business industries.

In this connection my recommendation is that, While a larger share of the CSR funds can be employed in the locale where the company is located, certain amount of the funds should be mandated to be spent on development of the **"backward districts"** as recognized by the Planning \Commission. However, this provision has already been made in *the "Guidelines on Corporate Social Responsibility and Sustainability for Central Public Sector Enterprises"*.

2. Section 135 of the 2013 Act should include 'Responsible business practices':

The first principle of corporate responsibility is not only to contribute to social development but to adopt a *responsible business practices* which includes ethical business practices, respect for human rights, fair sourcing and environmental responsibility. The National Voluntary Guidelines (NVGs) and United Nation Global Compact are based on these basic principles. Similarly, SEBI also mandates on this line that *"the top 100 companies have to report on the aforesaid principles i.e. ethical business practices, respect for human rights, fair sourcing and environmental responsibility in their Business Responsibility Reports"*. Nevertheless, the draft CSR rules repudiate these ideologies and give the idea of esteeming a company's 2% contribution for CSR initiatives more than the assessment of the company's respect for ethical practices, human rights and environmental responsibilities. This will not only provide a bad preference but project a one-sided image of Corporate Governance in India. Thus, by restricting the legal definition of CSR to community development, the government is not encouraging companies to assess and disclose their more substantive environmental, social and governance (ESG) impacts.

Thus, the Ministry Corporate Affairs should mandate on the line of SEBI dictate that all corporations impending under the purview of section 135 must develop specific policies on ethical business practices, respect for human rights, fair sourcing and environmental responsibility and report their observance to same, and any violation to this should be appropriately punishable.

3. CSR initiative Activities not exclusively for employees or their families should be considered as

CSR rules state that activities providing "Exclusive" benefit to employees and their families will not be considered as CSR. This provision requires further explanation as some benefit to the local community, can also result in the activity being listed as CSR activity. For example, capital and running expenditure of schools for children of employees with a few children from local community can also be termed as CSR. It can also happen for healthcare facilities and hospitals created by the company.

In this connection my submission is that, the employee and their family benefit to any CSR activity should be taken up may be in a limited way from the companies' total expenditure.

4. Establishing of self-Implementing Agencies for CSR practices:

CSR rules inspire companies to implement their CSR activities by establishing their own trust/ society or companies. However, deep-seated progressive issues are often multifarious and local civil society groups with presence in the local area for years recognize the peculiar matters and their solutions better than anyone else does. Many of them also operate in a larger context of social justice than on a project activity basis. It is beneficial both for the business houses and for the local community to partner with such a local organizations for better results and their impact.

Thus, at least 50 % of the CSR funds should be channelized to work through local development organizations not created by the companies in order to implement planned activities. Thus, on the same principle of appointment of the independent directors on the Company board as per the draft rule of CSR, company promoted trusts/ society/ companies also should not be headed by any of the employees or their family members or any CSR related donations should not be given to any trust/ society/companies sponsored by any employee or his/ her family members.

5. Timeline of CSR projects

The very policy of spending 2 % of net profit on CSR activities in a financial year should not lead to the practice of investing in projects which have a timeline of one year. Social development projects are often multifaceted with long incubation periods and take time to yield sustainable changes.

Thus it is recommend that, at least 60 % of CSR funds should be invested in projects aiming at brining long term sustainable socio-economic changes.

6. Fair Credit Reporting Act regulation

As per the **Fair Credit Reporting Act** regulations, any CSR contribution to an Indian organization from a foreign owned company would be treated as FCRA money. The same applies to donations from Indian companies in which foreign investors hold 51% or more ownership. Looking at the free movement of capital in a globalized world and thus ownership holding of a company, it might become difficult for many development organizations receiving CSR donations from *Indian Companies* to track their ownership/ shareholding. It might lead to a frequent involuntary FCRA violations and litigations.

On this important issue my suggestion is that, the Foreign ownership of the company at the end of the preceding financial year should be considered while deciding on the Indian or foreign nature of a company. This issue needs to be looked into and appropriate guidance may be issued.

7.Inclusion of penal provisions:

The Act does not prescribe any penal provision if a company fails to spend amount on CSR activities. The Board will need to explain reasons for non-compliance in its report. Thus, in order to bring strict implementations of the CSR policies as per the provisions specified in the Companies Act, 2013, the Act must include a penal provision for non-compliance of this mandatory CSR policy.

8. Failure to include companies below 500 crores net profits:

The Act clearly make a classifications of the companies by including only companies having 500 crores net profit and 1000 crores of trun over for CSR practices. Thus, it does not articulate about the companies having a net profit ranging from 100 crores to 400 crores. Therefore, the Act needs to be discussed on this very point.

CONCLUSION:

Since companies cannot act in any wider interest than the interest of profit, CSR is of limited use in creating social change. Since CSR is also a vehicle for companies to thwart attempts to control corporate power and to gain access to markets. Thus, it can be concluded that "The business of business is business." This view eschews **corporate social responsibility** for the maximization of profits, whereby society would be the indirect beneficiary of market capitalism. Organization in present world cannot be successful without taking into account the **social responsibility.** CSR has been a vital component for any organization to have perpetual success and to create brand.

In the age of globalized world, the concept of CSR can't be ignored by the corporate firms. By keeping in mind the changing market scenario business firms have to change their work culture as per the market demands. Previously we were fighting for the issues like labour laws, factory acts and child labour. But we can see the paradigm shift in the relation of corporate house and workers. Now a day's Firms and workers all together work as a family and work for achieving the common goals. Profit sharing is the main .agenda of the corporate houses. Those days have gone when basic business of business is to earn profits only.

CSR has become increasingly important to companies/ businesses over the last few years, with more and more companies responding to stakeholders' calls for increased accountability by incorporating and integrating CSR into their organization/business policies. In time, the public is likely to become increasingly discriminating, less willing to take general claims on trust, and more keen to see specific action. In this case, if companies are to maintain their standing and stake out leadership in the future,

As already discussed that the concept of Corporate Social Responsibility is not new to India, for example there are certain large companies such as Tata, Infosys and Mahindra & Mahindra are active participants when it comes to CSR activities, the performance of India Inc. has not been very impressive when it comes to taking up CSR initiatives. Even though Reliance India Limited is the largest CSR spender amongst Indian companies, even then its expenditure does not amount to 2% of the Profit after Taxes (PAT), as will be required under the Companies Bill, 2011. According to a survey carried out by Forbes India, only 6 out of the top 100 companies of India (ranked on the basis of net sales figures) contributed more than 2% of their profits after taxes towards CSR initiatives. Also, only 16 out of the top 100 companies published a separate Sustainability Report for the financial year 2011-2012.

Similarly, a study indicates that 60% of the participants of the Global Compact Society (GCS), India's equivalent of the United Nations Global Compact (UNGC), had not submitted a 'Communication on Progress' or COP Report, which is the UN's version of a Sustainability Report by the company, stating the various CSR initiatives taken by it for the benefit of its various stakeholder. However, the new CSR rules as inserted in the Companies Act 2013, which made a clear demarcations of the companies are somewhat not rational as it clearly make a classifications by including the companies with 500 crore net profits and excluding the companies underneath this line. Thus, the Act remains silence on this point and does not bother about the companies having a net worth from 100 crores to 400 crores.

Insipte of the aforesaid drawbacks the major advantage of mandating CSR spending, as opposed to levying additional taxes, would be the preservation of the company's autonomy in selecting how its funds are used. To some extent, the corporation would be "free" to invest its funds in the community directly or in a local non-profit or national NGO. Companies could use the money to further minimize externalities, beyond the requirements of environmental law, or they could choose to create positive externalities by building schools or providing workers with more comprehensive benefits. Knowing that each corporation might bring two percent of its profits to the community for re-investment, community members might be far more enthusiastic about the potential of industry coming to their neighborhood. *As Tom Tyler and Peter Degoey note, re-investing in communities can build reputational legitimacy, trust, and reciprocity from which companies may ultimately benefit.201 If community members and other stakeholders feel that the company is extending its fiduciary duty to encompass their well-being, then they may feel some positive duty to act in the company's best interest in return. Similarly, local residents who have been treated well by the company—educated in its school or nursed in its hospital—are less likely to organize protests and create extra costs when and if the company does make a mistake.*

Companies in India, perhaps because of incidents like Bhopal and Dabhol, already seem eager, when they do engage in CSR spending, to create positive externalities that would be recognized and appreciated by the local community. Most companies that have CSR programs (around fifty-six percent) spend their money locally.[2] The vast majority invest in education (eighty-two percent) or health (eighty-one percent).[3] Spending on the environment is also popular.[4] It seems odd, however, that environmental spending does not rank higher given the Bhopal incident and the fact that environmental disasters can have such terrible reputational and fiscal consequences. Schools and hospitals, however, may simply engender more recognition, reciprocity, and good-will in communities since they are much more visible than the efforts a company takes to prevent negative externalities. In the end, companies may find this trust and good-will more valuable than traditional risk-prevention. Thus, it may be concluded that state-driven corporate social responsibility cuts against the thrust of most current CSR practice and scholarship, which generally focus on voluntary business-driven initiatives and international agreements. Nevertheless, as the popularity of CSR surges, more and more national and international players will be seeking to harness the power of corporate-funded investment in social welfare projects. Accordingly, India's state-based proposal may represent merely the beginning of a new wave of development in the realm of corporate social responsibility. A product of unique historical exigencies, the proposal may represent a new type of solution to an increasingly pressing international problem.

It is better described by the **Niall Fitzerald, Former CEO, Unilever** that - *"Corporate social responsibility is a hard-edged business decision. Not because it is a nice thing to do or because people are forcing us to do it... because it is good for our business"*[5]

[1] *National Foundation for India, COMMENTS ON DRAFT CSR RULES UNDER SECTION 135 OF COMPANIES ACT, available at www.nfi.org.in/ sites/.../**Comments%20on%20draft%20CSR%20rules**.pdf*

[2] TIMES FOUNDATION, *supra* note 16, at 12.

[3] ibid

[4] ibid

[5] Aniket Pandey, Corporate Social Responsibility And Its Enforceability

Bibliograhy:

1. Archie B. Carroll, "The Pyramid of Corporate Social Responsibility: Towards the Moral Management of Organizational Stakeholders", Business Horizons, July-August, 1991, p40. (www.sciencetarget.com).
2. Bowen, H.R. (1953),"Social responsibilities of businessman", New York: Harper & Row.
3. Business Ethics and Corporate Governance, ICFAI Publications, 2008.
4. Business for Social Responsibility. 2003b. Overview of Corporate Social Responsibility.
5. Commission of the European Communities, availableat\:http://ec.europa.eu/ index_en.htm(accessed 14 February 2009).
6. Corporate Social Responsibility – Perceptions of Indian Business. Available at:www.csmworld.org/public/pdf/ social_respons.pdf
7. Chapter IX of the Draft Rules (First Phase) under Companies Act, 2013, Ministry of Corporate Affairs.
8. CSR Report Card: Where Companies Stand, Forbes India, Mar. 18, 2013 available at http://forbesindia.com/article/real-issue/csr-report-card-where-companies stand/34893/1.
9. India Inc. needs to wake up to its social responsibilities, Forbes India, Mar. 18, 2013 available at http://forbesindia.com/article/boardroom/india-inc-needs-to-wake-up-to-its-social responsibilities/ 34891/ 1.
10. Companies bill 2009, twenty first report by ministry of **corporate** affairs, www.tpcc.in/Downloads/

company%20bill.htm

11. Dahl R A (1972); A prelude to corporate reform; Business & Society Review, Spring 1972, 17-23

12. Freidman, Milton, "Capitalism and Freedom," University of Chicago Press, 1962, p133.

13. Frederick W, Post J, Davis KE.1992. Business and Society. Corporate Strategy, Public Policy, Ethics, 7th edn. McGraw-Hill: London.

14. Global Corporate Social Responsibility Policies Project. 2003. A Role for the Government – Issues at Hand, Kenan-Flagler Business School of the University of North Carolina,ChapelHill.http://www.csrpolicies.org/CSRRoleGov/CSR_Issue/csr_issue.html [20 May 2003].

15. Hopkins M.1998. The Planetary Bargain: Corporate Social Responsibility Comes of Age. Macmillan: London

16. "Issue Brief: Overview of Corporate Social Responsibility". Business for Social Responsibility Website

17. IssueBriefDetail.cfm?DocumentID=48809 [23 June 2003].

18. Kakabadse, N.K. Rozuel, C. and Lee-Davies, L. (2005) 'Corporate social responsibility and stakeholder approach: a conceptual review', *Int. J. Business Governance and Ethics*, Vol. 1, No. 4, pp.277–302

19. Khoury G, Rostami J, Turnbull JP. 1999. Corporate Social Responsibility: Turning Words into Action. Conference Board of Canada: Ottawa.

20. Kotler Philip and Lee Nancy, Corporate SocialResponsibility: Doing the most Good for Your Company, John Wiley and Sons, Inc. New Jersey **(2005)**

21. Levitt, 1958; Friedman, 1970; Lantos, 2001; Drucker, 2001; Porter and Kramer, 2006; Meehan et al., 2006.

(Bhattacharyya, 2008). Willam B. Werther, JR.& David Chandler, University of Maimi, ' Strategic Corporate Social Responsibility, Stakeholders in global environment,pp10-11.

22. McWilliams, A. and Siegel, D. (2001), "Corporate responsibility: a theory of the firm perspective", The Academy of Management Review, Vol. 26, No. 1, pp. 117–127.

23. Michael Porter and Mark Kramer, Harvard Business Review, Dec., 2006

24. Ministry of Corporate Affairs, Corporate Social Responsibility Voluntary Guidelines, 2009 available at http://www.mca.gov.in/Ministry/latestnews/ CSR_Voluntary_Guidelines_24dec2009.pdf.

25. NCERT, *Business Studies for Class XI*, 143-144, (8th Edition Revised)

26. OECD Guidelines for Multinational Enterprises, available at: http://actrav.itcilo.org/actrav-english/ telearn /global/ilo/guide/oecd.htm (accessed 30 January 2009).

27. S. Ravi, FCA, Overview of Corporate Social Responsibility

28. published in 1953 (Valor, 2005)

29. Press Information Bureau, Ministry of Petroleum and Natural Gas, Government of India, Oil PSUs agrees to spend two per cent of profits on Social Responsibilities, Feb. 2, 2009 available at http://pib.nic.in/newsite/ erelease.aspx?relid=47172.

30. Press Information Bureau, Ministry of Corporate Affairs, Government of India, Corporate Social Responsibility, 11 Aug. 2011 available at http://pib.nic.in/newsite/erelease.aspx?relid=74428.

31. Rajeev Prabhakar and Ms. Sonam Mishra (2013) "A

BIBLIOGRAHY:

Study of Corporate Social Responsibility in Indian Organization: An-Introspection",International Business Research Conference, Ryerson University, Toronto, Canada

32. Social responsibility of Businessmen (P.12)
33. THE EVOLUTION OF CORPORATE SOCIAL RESPONSIBILITY (CSR) IN INDIA, Source: Indian Streams Research Journal (ISSN:-2230-7850) yr:2013 vol:3 iss:5,
34. The Challenges of Social Corporate Social Responsibility: Facts for You, May 2013, pp. 38-39. India, Ministry of Corporate Affairs, Corporate Social Responsibility Voluntary Guidelines 2009.
35. TIMES FOUNDATION, *supra* note 16, at 12.
36. World Business Council for Sustainable Development. 1999. Corporate Social Responsibility: Meeting Changing Expectations. World Business Council for Sustainable Development: Geneva

<u>WEBLIOGRAPHY</u>

37. www.mca.gov.in/Ministry/**companies_act**.html
38. http://response.restoration.noaa.gov/photos/exxon.html
39. [1] http://www.organicconsumers.org/corp/monprotest.cfm
40. [1] Campaigns: Corporates, http://www.foe.co.uk/campaigns/corporates/index.html
41. http://www.csrpolicies.org/CSRRoleGov/CSR_Issue/csr_issue.html [20 May 2003].
42. http://www.bsr.org/BSRResources/
43. http://www.unido.org/what-we-do/trade/csr/what-*is-csr.html#pp1[g1]/0/*

44. http://ec.europa.eu/enterprise/policies/
sustainable-*business/corporate-social*   *responsibility/*
index_ en.htm

45. http://www.bombaychamber.com/image002.jpg

46. http://www.bsr.org/CSRResources/
IssueBriefDetail.cfm?DocumentID=48809

47. **www.isrj.net**

48. http://www.corporatewatch.org.uk/?lid=2682,   the
evolution of CSR

49. http://www.pwc.com

50. www.legalservices**india**.com/.../the-**bhopal-gas-tragedy**-on-
whether-and

51. www.mmbgims.com/docs/ppt/31.ppsx